THE EXALTING HEIGHTS

Stories of my Himalayan Adventures

ANIL WINDIE

INDIA • SINGAPORE • MALAYSIA

ISBN 979-8-88869-030-7

"So the Himalaya remains to us a joy of which we never tire. The ill is but the evanescent. What stays for always with us is the grandeur, purity and light. And these have power to draw us ever lasting to heaven."

Sir Francis Younghusband

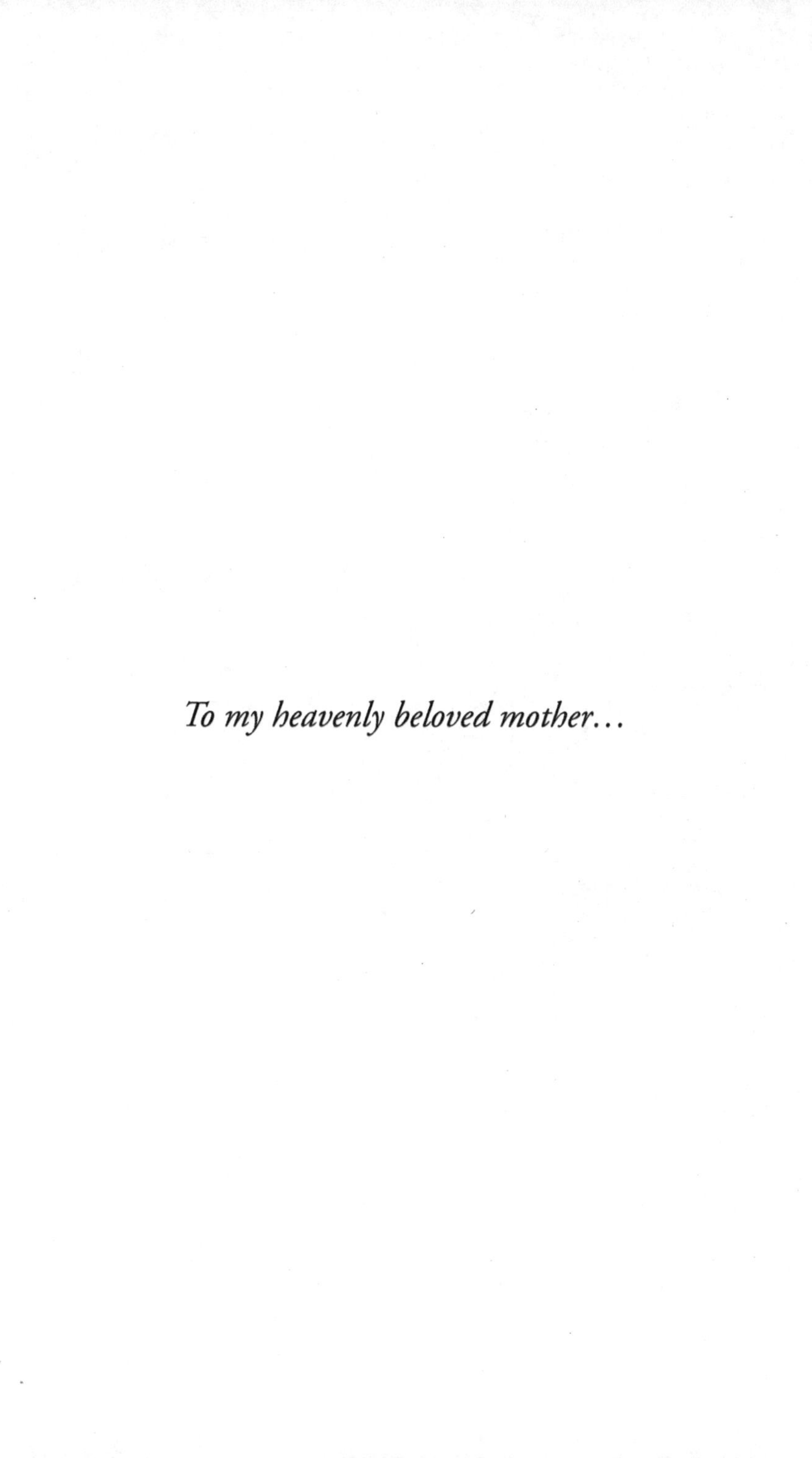

To my heavenly beloved mother…

Contents

Author's Note

The genesis of this book started in the year 2019. Initially, every event was noted in my routine almanac on day to day basis. A few blogs on some expeditions were published online. However lately; on constant request of some adventure loving friends, I started to scribble each story chapter wise. All of the events are my first hand experience, however name of a few persons and places are changed in order to keep the anonymity and privacy. A few references have been drawn from some adventure books and online publication as well. Most of the stories are from Himachal Himalaya as I myself is endemic to this place. The conservation of Nature and its habitat is also taken up in few chapters. The events mentioned are not in chronological order.

Hope the readers will enjoy these adventure tales and find themselves intrepid in wilderness with me.

Himachal Himalaya Rough Sketch (Not to Scale)

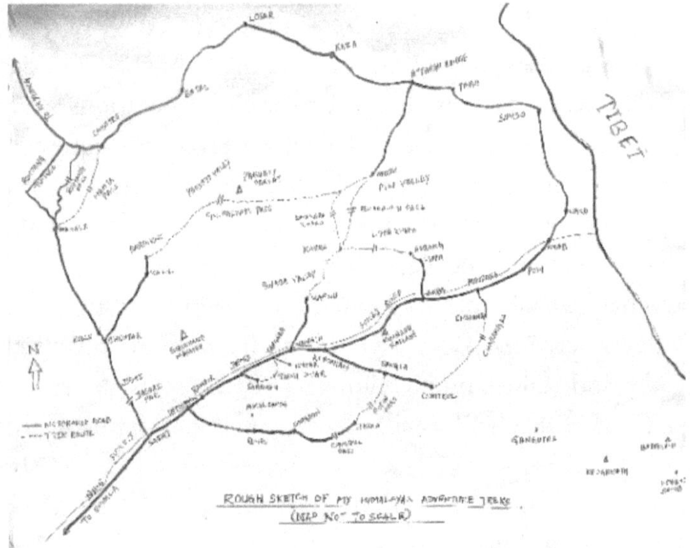

Introduction

"At the foothill of high Outer Himalayan ranges, near the basin of river Sutlej, I wonder how human desires have belittled the enormity of these mountains. Nor do the desires quell with final assault but it only increases for repeating the same with double resolution".

Finally monsoon has entered this part of the world. For past two-three days it's raining intermittently. The charm of monsoon aura is unique in itself, for one may feel lost amid wafting fog and looming mist shrouding all the beauty of nature around. Temperature becomes soothingly bearable after scorching summer heat. It's also gala time for all living beings be it Kingdom *Animalia or*Kingdom *Plantae* as the rain brought new life, new hope to these organisms which survived chances of desiccation and decimation in hot dry summer. Drought is overwhelmed. Various flowers blossom not only in the nicely manicured backyard but also on high altitude alpine pastures making it the best time to visit these vistas which are full of life these days. Ethereal feeling of fog growing and dwindling around; makes one euphoric to extreme. Besotted beauty of motley colored *bugyals* interspersed with myriad wild flowers only get embellished in this season.

But it's not the perfect season for hikers like me; as we are not much concerned about topping the hill but to enjoy the aura around and the beautiful journey through the foothills. Monsoon is not the recommended season to scale a mountain for the risk involved are always high, also these monsoon rain only add to the perils; landslides, thunderstorms, lighting and cloudburst are common in this season. Every year some bad news is heard on social or print media regarding loss of life or property due to natural calamity that is bound to happen during this season.

In 2018 *Kinnaur Kailash Yatra* which is organized by the Kinnaur administration for fifteen days, beginning from August 1st in the holy month of *Saawan,* ought to be cancelled after instances of heavy landslides were observed and it was hard time for administration to conduct rescue operations at such heights, that also in constantly bad weather. Many times the holy *Shrikhand MahadevYatra* in Kullu district had also been cancelled officially midway due to bad weather. So a brief halt is all that is needed during this 30 to 45 days, but how can this ingenious, highly infatuated mind be tamed and that also for that long!

I like and follow the tenets of many explorers and mountaineers who believe safety to be first priority, fun second and success third. There is always a next time, but then how to sit comfortably in good shape back at home throughout monsoon?

I got myself engrossed in high altitude mountaineering books and on adventure storieswhich I devoured exhaustively, *Touching the void*, *No Shortcuts to the Top*, *Alone on the wall*, *Walking the Himalayas*, *Eager Dreams* etc. to name a few. In most of these expedition accounts certain themes and attitudes towards wild landscape recur. Foremost among is that of victory and defeat, of struggle and reward. In these books nature is figured usually as a lover, or an enemy, to be ravished or vanquished according to how you saw it. This only filliped the flickering desire of wandering in the mountains, introspecting and enjoying the nature around. How miniscule one feel under these hercules creation of nature and so does our ego!

I am 37 years and 7 months old, and for now seems to be in perfect health condition. I get up around 5.00 am every morning and enjoy an average 5 km jog along National Highway-05 and thereafter the mandatory calisthenics session. My daily routine is a bit constant now for past 2-3 years. No sign of any pain, strain or sprain observed as of now. I am an avid hiker, though not climbed any big peak. In fact I must not categorize myself as a 'mountain climber' at all. I don't know the basics of climbing, nor did I own any paraphernalia for high altitude mountaineering. But I may be considered as a '*five thousander*' and I am content with it.

Someone has rightly said, *'Placing one foot in front of other gives meaning to our lives, directing us to what lies ahead. It is as fundamental to human nature as opposable thumb or the pleasure we feel at moment of orgasm. Walking is a ritual that recognizes the divinity in nature what animal have known forever, the indefinable footfalls of being. Every walk in the wild becomes a prayer'*.

Human desires to scale highest peaks never die. Only yesterday, came down from the high altitude pasture after conquering the highest peak above this pasture measuring

4300 meters above sea level; post three days outing, what I call an 'expedition'. It's always but natural that in harsh scorching summer, people want to get some respite by moving up to higher altitude. In last two-three summers I made it a motto that I should scale 2-3 hills, if not the big mountains. To me the big ones were *Shrikhand Mahadev* peak in Distt. Kullu, *Kinnaur Kailash* Peak and *Charang La,* both in Kinnaur District of Himachal Pradesh. All stood above 5000 meters mark. This year being the worst in human history, for it is largely marred by COVID Pandemic, the goals regarding summer sojourn won't be fulfilled. So I decided to hike local pastures that in turn would fetch two benefits. One, that it would be an official tour with regard to disease surveillance in livestock grazing at high alpine pasture and second, the livestock owner would be equally happy to see some Govt. official taking care of their livestock, at such remote terrain.

The peak that we conquered recently above *Taranda* village, Kinnaur, was quite a broad peak, rightly called as *Jhotte ki Nakri* (Back of a male buffalo) by local nomad *gujjars*, just above the top of *Chhonda Nullah* past *Nigulsari* bridge, Kinnaur (my place of posting). It's still covered with white glaciers, commanding a blissful view right from my spartan shanty, enough to entice any hiker. During my stay here at *Nigulsari*, for past more than two and a half year I had nurtured a hidden dream to be at its top some day. And now, for my tenure is about to expire by next summer, and given the present pandemic conditions, this was the perfect time to assault… and the bliss up above was well beyond explicitly.

(Kinnaur, 2019)

Man and Exploration

Human being, *Homo sapiens sapiens* has always found a gene in its DNA since the 'cognitive revolution' started centuries ago to explore and find new things in its surroundings. Initially it was for its own survival; be it for hunting or gathering the food material; that gene has always inherited through the evolutionary history of this species.

We all like exploration, which may differ in intensity but excitement of venturing out and looking for new things persists. In the due course of time, while many civilizations perished but the search for new things continued.

It's not about exploring the extreme things, be it the two poles or the greatest heights in the Himalayas but even something as small as deep gorge or parched land or a sand dune surrounding one's habitat. Some of the creature made it a passion and some even made it profession. Those who are busy with their other means of livelihood are equally enticed by discoveries that were made by eccentrics, as they were called, or are still considered even today. It was only due to this human nature of exploration that many civilizations thrived and prospered. In past 1000 years or so the geo-political maps has changed a lot due to such nature of exploration. Had the westerners contained the zeal to explore; perhaps the intellectual development of the Sapiens would not have been the same that we do appreciate today. Daring task it must have been when a few explorers headed to unknown sea or land, putting their life at stake, even many perished away never to come back again. But that spirit of exploration never ended. Another generation would come up with utmost zeal and took the place of old ones with great vigor and much better prepared than their predecessors, learning a lot from the experiences of past. This gene of exploration brought the *Homo sapiens* on the top of pyramid and became the master of this planet.

In *Mountains of the Mind*, Robert Macfarlane has rightly described,

'The concept of unknownhas not always possessed and allure in and of itself. For centuries the chief incentive for exploration were economic, political and egotistical one; the desire for money, territory or glory. The unknown *per se* held no allure; wise explorers plotted out their journeys on the maps of the familiar. Once again it was the later eighteenth century, which incubated the longing for the unknown in western imagination. During the second half of 1700s in Europe, there emerged a new and distinctive appetite for remote countries, for different territories, taste and sensation – for orders of experience we might now call exotic, meaning literally *on the outside*, in short; for discovery……The unknown came to be seen as a gateway to these alternative orders of experience.

Charles Baudelaire put it well several decades later: *"Au fondde l'Inconnu pour trouver du nouveau";* Through the unknown, we will find the new.

In recent times more enthusiasm was observed to explore the highest peaks of different mountain ranges. It was not just about conquering the top most natural thing in the surroundings, but people did ventured out hundreds and thousands of kilometers to some unknown land just to be on the top of this world. For some the solace and serenity that these mountains provide cannot be replaced with any other work of contentment.

Once a Swiss naturalist, Conrad Gessner wrote, *'From the Alpine mountain top, wrote a, one might observe on a single day four season of the year'.*

Himalayas are often regarded and described as the place of solace and *Nirvana*, even in Hindu's ancient texts of *Vedas* and *Puranas.* Sages and seers used to venture out in these remote mountain ranges in search of the God and seeking *Nirvana*, which still continue even at this point of time. Spirituality has always thrived through these treacherous and bewildering creations of nature. For many explorers, not just reaching the top is the sole motto but the journey in itself is worth finding penance or to explore within. The sense of accomplishment and achievement that one apprehend while being on the top is something worth putting hard work for.

Poet John Keats wrote that, *at height; a new creation burst upon our site.*

The summit and the slopes leading to it, provide the visible goal and the challenge respectively. The resolution that one achieve after reaching the set goal only get bolster up with each peak conquered. One experiences a strange emotion in the remote mountains, on discovering the living words that he/ she have read in the pages of distant book.

More over once being on the top, all the things downstream looks small and diminutive like all other miseries of life. The hardship that one dwells throughout the journey seems to be all gone, in the extreme excitement and euphoria that one apprehends after being on the top. An explorer remains *terra firma* for he knew the truth of life and is ignorant about the mystiques of social life. Someone has truly said that an explorer is in love either with oneself or with the oblivion.

When you are on an expedition the only worry is about one's survival. Lesser the number of an expedition members more the inner self you explore, for it is only you and yourself which work in tandem for the sole purpose of survival. This sheer sense of survival had been the only force which steered the *Homo sapiens* to present status.

At top, icy solitude is appreciable; the stillness of death apprehended. What one hearsis one's own breathing sound and sonorous heartbeats. But still people ascend to bare heights to romanticize the barrenness and sterility of such aura. Robert Macfarlane has rightly put it out that you could be lonely in a city crowd but you could find solitude on mountain top. As some French philosopher has said the 'leap' is a basic form of joy.

On reaching a summit, reward is not only in terms of 'far sight' but 'in site' as well. Not only landscape, but also mindscape is revealed to those who conquer the summit. Someone says height appeals only to those who are hiking freaks, but then be this the case, why do people throng to enjoy cable car or timber trolley uphill?

In present digital era the importance of seeking solitude had increased many folds. Perhaps new generation cannot even imagine about living a reclusive life, and what for? Self introspection is not a great term anymore. But then as experiences have it, in this virtual digital life more resolute and self contained one ought to be. And that sense of accomplishment and fulfillment, may probably be developed through such austere but blissful mountaineering. When you are devoid of any, so called luxuries, irritated you may feel initially but then that basic instinct of survival takes over and all other comforts looks secondary. This pristine feeling rose to apex while being on the top and one do mingle only with the serene nature around. Every breath of pure fresh air seems so precious and one find itself quite insignificant in front of mother nature, leave behind the sense of being at top of pyramid and master of all creatures.

Rumbling sounds from some breaking scree would be audible at times and some deafening sound of ice; breaking from glacier's snout may be enough to apprehend the mightyness and cruelness of this nature, reminding oneself the ephemeral life of egoist Sapiens.

The eagerness to explore the unknown by Sapiens will continue not only in term of physical world but spiritual and rapidly progressing digital world as well, for the 'exploration' gene will perpetuate till last living being.

Mental Status: Pre & Post Expedition

InAugust 2020, after our small party marched up *Bhaba Valley,* Kinnaur, and not only reached the *Bhaba Pass*, but also explored further deep into *Tia Valley* and ascended up to *Lippa Pass*. It was a ten days expedition in total, and we were cut off from the outer world completely. Some excerpts from my daily diary, which illuminate the state of mind, thought process and considerations that a trekker undergo, before any expedition and the true feelings apprehended post –expedition.

Pre Expedition

12/08/2020 11.35 AM NIGULSARI, KINNAUR

Sitting on the doorstep of my office building, amid meticulously manicured flower beds, watching intently at the gushing majestic river Sutlej at the basin, I wonder what I shall get during proposed detour to *Bhaba* valley this weekend. Is it only for the solace and tranquility uphill or the sense of being much closer to Mother Nature? How different is it to be at social gregarious life than to be all alone in the wilderness?

The slow contemplative hiking between two places is a process of spiritual journeying, a time removed from everyday obligations, a brief period for introspection. Is this whole process of exploration much more important than its geographical goals? Or is it merely about showing the world that I am just another mountain wondering freak?

Perhaps the answers evolve in the meditation of walking and the openness that hardship induces.

After concluding all my personal obligations back at home, be it in the form of harvesting the apple crop, post-harvest orchard management, helping my little kid in his studies or sharing chores and love with my better half; I feel free to give some private moment to myself. My first expedition of the season was toward local *kanda*, *Dhar Tirmi*, Kinnaur, in the month of early June 2020, which got many accolades from friends through social media. Now it's time to head again towards alpine pasture. I missed the four high passes last month with seasoned guide Billu Wangpa due to some unavoidable reasons, but that ecstasy of being on the top still prevails. So I made a rough plan about *BhabaPass* again. All the members of my core hiking friends could not join because of their personal engagements but then I am so much obsessed with these mountains that I thought about giving it a solo try, again.

Moreover, I was engrossed in reading work '*No shortcut to the top*' by the legendry American mountaineer *Ed Viesturs*. All his fourteen 8000ers conquers have further fanned my reveries of being on some mountain; be it half the altitude. In fact I apprehended the thrill of climbing the top of the world vicariously but I also realize the fact that neither do I have the expertise of climbing a small hill nor do I have the physique and skills to conquer any. But all the while I wondered that the feeling of solace and serenity remains same whether one climb a 8000er or hike as low as half its altitude. The risk of topping a mountain may vary according to its elevation but the preparations are almost similar for each.

If one takes part in a full marathon his preparations are guided in a much concentrated manner than to a person who take part in a mini marathon of say 15 kilometers but the thrill that one experience during any of these remains the same. So is true about mountaineering. What if someone do not climb a seriously technical and arduous mountain but only a small hill in his/ her back door, but the rush of adrenaline remains the same. None the less topping each kind of height brings bliss equivalently irrespective of the altitude gained.

So it is again about venturing towards picturesque *Bhaba* valley, that I had explored many a times. Desperate I was to the extent that I finalized the days tentatively and thought about heading all alone, in case no one joins. Fortunately this time Dr Ankush, a local Vet at *Urni*, Kinnaur showed his desire to move along. We both had been to *Bhaba* valley before, to attend a disease outbreak two years ago. Though, his thoughts of hiking may be guided by the fantasies of being on the top of an alpine pasture, but as I said earlier, the ecstasies are always equivalent.

As usual I chalked out the itinerary at my disposal and forwarded it to him, to which he agreed instantaneously. This time more focus will be over flora and fauna of that terrain. I have brought two tents along, one a small *Two men tent* (courtesy Pawan Johnny, my younger brother) and another regular *Three men plus quechua* tent. So, if no one else gives a confirmation by this evening we will carry small, light weighted *Two men tent.* I also bought a kerosene stove to quell all the doubts of cooking meals at high alpine pastures and up above tree line. Last time when we explored *Dhar Tirmi*, we hauled the old worn out office kerosene-stove along. Though it was working well in downhill but gave away in *Tirmi* top. We tried our best to keep it in working conditon, by covering the stove to prevent fierce winds or pumping it to utmost limit.

Finally after toiling for more than a couple of hours we decided to make a fire. Luckily we had camped just above tree line, so easily collected the dwarf rhododendron firewood and made dinner. Was it due to dilapidated condition of *Kero*-stove or lack of oxygen but the truth remain that we could not make food over stove that night.

This time brand new stove is working well here, hope it would work like that up above.

To me it would be a nine days sojourn and I left the decision to others for their journey. Standard itinerary is for four days. We will try to top the *Bhaba* pass on day three and then head back very next day. I would loiter around the valley for next four days.

Provisions and ration has been calculated on daily meal basis. More the number of members less load we have to haul. In my view every member has to carry at least fifteen kilograms of load up to *Karra* pasture. I am resolute to haul my load all the way up, though couldn't guarantee others. Menu has been crafted on daily basis, and final adjustments will be made on the spot. I hope it will be a clear weather next week.

15th August was chosen to be at *Karra* pasture, more so about memorizing my solo effort up *Bhaba-Pin* Pass two years ago. Till then I was not confident whether I could make it all alone, but it happened and rest is all history.

There was also corona COVID scare at the base of this (*Bhaba*) valley. A few people has tested positive three days ago, containment zone has been declared, fortunately only around their homes. Had it been the whole valley as rumor had it, it would have been a bit tough call. Though again we were moving on the pretext of attending a disease outbreak in ovine flock, up above. When else shall our essential services pay us more than free movement during such times?

My backpack was almost ready. I washed all my hiking attire, oiled my gears, charged my batteries and loaded my gun (I wish I had an original one). The hiking season for the year was about to culminate to its end by September fifteenth, as it would be cold to venture out thereafter, and we are just small creatures to come out of our cocoons for a short period, to show other's that we are the real mountaineers!

I wished I could have joined a big professional expedition this year, but alas! Corona scare washed all the hopes down the drain. Anyways, self introspection and appraisal need not to be done only during some serious climbing. It's here, within, always. It's all about fun and enjoyment. Life is too short. May be *the next time* will never come, so never say 'Never'.

13.08.2020 8.43 PM NIGULSARI, KINNAUR

"Mountains are not conquered and should be treated with respect and humility. If we take what the mountain gives, have patience and desire, and are prepared, the mountain will permit to reach their highest peaks. I believe a lot of things are like that in life."Ed Vistures, No shortcut to top.

Finally the rucksack lies packed in one of the corner of my small rented room at *Nigulsari*, Kinnaur. All the needed accessories that I've minutely listed before smotheringit down through the narrow top of my trusted backpack, a strange feeling prevails all through the day, before actually starting the journey. Arranging the things and leading the troop is always a thanklessly cumbersome job, but the reassurance that one gets after putting everything in order is inexplicable. I again today scrutinized the list of provisions and ration. A little bit of adjustment was made for there was one more addition to our group, as Dr Pramod Mahajan our colleague lately joined the team.

Procurement of provisions has been delegated to Dr Ankush and transportation up to last motorable point will be looked after by TC (Tara Chand), our staffer and old trusted guy at *Katgaon, Bhaba valley,* Kinnaur. There was a little bit of tweaking with regard to original itinerary, as more positive cases of Corona COVID-19 erupted by this morning. It was probable that entire *Bhaba* valley may be considered as 'containment zone'. At one point of time when it was speculated that we had to abort the expedition, I started to work on Plan B.

I will head towards *Tirmi* top all alone and circumambulate through *Bari* and *Nichar Kanda*, for my rucksack was ready and the holidays won't be let wasted. However by evening we came to know that only *Yangpa* village across the *Bhaba* gorge has been declared as 'containment zone'.

I made a proposal that we start the hike tomorrow afternoon from *Katgaon* instead of staying at local guest house; which in fact was also difficult to be booked in such situation, and rather we should camp at *Humti*, a small knoll, just above the *Homte* village. It would take maximum of three hours to reach *Humti* camping site where most of the shepherds stay and use it as base camp before proceeding to high alpine pasture. There is a small stream beside the camp site and we could have gala time far beyond the scare of corona virus down the valley.

One more positive thing that took place today was, one of my subordinate staff succeeded in making contact with Billu Wangpa the veteran hiker, for he knew each and every nook and corner of this terrain like the back of his hand. I missed the chance to be with him last month when he along with his friend explored the four high passes of this valley before circumnavigating the *Bhaba-Pin* Pass. I was trying to get in touch with him with the hope that he may accompany us and we could take full advantage of his expertise. And surprised I was when I finally talked to him and he told that he fortunately found the signal only this very moment while hiking the *Khaanta* region, towards the top of *Karra*. He will be in this pasture for next fortnight, for the Corona scare down the valley has driven everyone up the mountains.

He seemed happy when I told him about my plans of exploring the valley. All other members would retreat once we try to make ascent up Bhaba-Pin Pass. He gingerly told that a deep picturesque valley on the left flank of *Karra* pasture leads all the way to *Lippa Kanda* after crossing a clandestine Pass. So were we trying to set our feet on it? I pondered!

We have got stove, tent and provisions. And most importantly the steel *Will* to be close to mother Nature, away from hustle and bustle of social scary life.

Jean Christophe Lafaille, a French mountaineer, has told a journalist while his attempt on Annapurna that,

"*after Roc Noir I had the feeling of closing the door behind me. I was far from the land of living.*"

Such feeling of '*closing the door*' for me has already started, well within my shanty and that also as early as the previous night of actual hike.

Also, one more good news of the day was that one of our staffer, a local guy, posted with departmental sheep farm, *Jeori* (Shimla), Mr Rajeshwar Negi heard the news of our proposed expedition and called me impromptu. He was also planning to move up to *Karra* tomorrow. So I asked him why not he joins us, to which he agreed. This fellow is a thorough gentleman and equally courteous, who in my solo attempt of *Bhaba-Pin* Pass, few years ago, accompanied me up to top and also arranged for my further journey. Moreover he is my schoolmate and I had always enjoyed his trusted company. So overall it's a good thing altogether.

Departure time has been fixed 1 p.m. from *Katgaon*, our base camp. We would stop briefly at *Bhaba* valley for its better to minimize the contact over there. This feeling of relinquishing everything is all that is needed and can't be explained.

Finally a sigh of relief and freedom! Well it would be my second Independence Day celebration at high alpine pasture. The folk camping there love and admire the guests coming from down hills, with the hope that they will bring the locally brewed potion. I still remember the way we celebrated till late night, on same day; two years ago, even when an early march was scheduled next morning to reach the Pass on time. So is it a *Deja vu*? Only time will tell. But at least we won't be in a hurry to assault the pass very next morning this time.

Post Expedition

23.08.2020 10.50 AM BHARASA (KOTGARH, SHIMLA)

A strange sense of intoxication swath me all around. I am unmoved to any other excitement or sorrows. A kind of utmost serenity and extreme calmness is appreciable. Ear keep on buzzing with slight din even when river *Sutlej* is far-far away from my place. Every thought is that about wilderness. I find no interest in getting hold of my cell phone. I am highly irritated whenever the phone rings up. Social media has lost its interest. I don't find any charm in reading old stories of either *Facebook* or *WhatsApp*. It's a kind of new life all together, even when period of my sojourn was just around 10 days. How calm, how blessed I felt, as I lay in a state of almost prophetic trance and delight.

While on my journey back to home I was asking the co-passengers about latest news of the world? What was happening in the society? To what extent Corona COVID scare has elevated? What was the progress of remedial measures?

In my dreams I was again gaily wandering through the shepherd's hovel. I revel the frolic banters of these nomads, the pranks that they made as early as 4 a.m, the hardship and daunting task of traversing a steep crag or crossing a deafening glacial gorge.

I am just sitting beside one of the corner of my home, in a kind of frozen state. All I am thinking about is the beautiful serene aura of high Himalayan land. It's but natural as many hikers and trekkers move through such state of mind after the journey is over.

Yesterday came all the way back to home after a brief halt at my office. I enquired about official updates. I was told that due to heavy rainfall, power supply was hampered and it would take some time to restore it. So there was no point in going to my rented shanty. I washed my stinking filthy clothes inside office washroom. Tap water was soothingly hot in comparison to that of glacial stream in which I took bath nine days ago. I shaved my grayish-black stubble with the help of my mobile *selfie* (no mirror facility at my office), trimmed my long dirty nails and within half an hour I was a completely different man, though apparently; well acceptable to so called civilized society. How easy is it to change outward than to change within? A real challenge indeed!

I reached home late evening after visiting the construction site of my new house, where the mason howled, as if I had gone missing for long. I found no difference in running the whole world around in my absence. Neighbors were busy in their routine work, kids playing in oblivion, traffic running as usual, hustle and bustle of bazaar having no change and shopkeepers busy in making their profits. Friends also changed their topics after a brief chats on me and my expeditions. Even family members were now giving more importance to other household chores.

It is a bitter truth that, my or for that matter anybody's presence or absence hardly makes a difference in this world. Things keep running at its own pace.

Then why we are so much concerned about others all the while? Human beings have evolved through the hard blows of fight to survive. It is deep in its genes.

Everything is forgettable, nothing indispensable.

Happiness isn't a truth-too absolute a noun. Peace might serve as a suitable synonym, though it leads in far too many directions. Happiness is a transient emotion that can arise out of discipline and meditation but more often, surprise us at moments when we expect it least.

On a mountain top, suddenly dark clouds of anger or distress, and the opaque mists of depression left to reveal a blissful panorama of the valleys below; that reduce our human agony to insignificant proportion.

Now I understand that terrible things happen on beautiful places just as beautiful things in terrible places. Yet, I was alive and grateful to be back.

On the other hand post-jaunt; like always, dear better half is taking care of my worn out clothes and unserviceable paraphernalia, while mumbling invectives intermittently. She hates my sudden disappearance but then somehow again keep my rucksack and equipments well polished and tidy. Is it due to her sheer love and devotion or does she takes it as her moral duty?

I acknowledge that due to my selfish sojourns I have always given very little time to my family than they deserve, but then this whole world is selfish in one way or the other. I always try to keep the things on an even keel till the next expedition begins…

Exploring Marvellous *Taranda Dhank*

The most thrilling moment that I enjoy while entering the tribal district Kinnaur in Himachal Pradesh is at the very beginning border point of *Chaura*. Shortly the terrain starts to turn perilous with steep big boulders flanking both sides of National Highway-05. The real adrenaline rush occurs while crossing treacherously famous *Taranda Dhank*. Asia's architectural marvel as it has been is made by simple manual work in the mid 60's. A small temple of *Maa Durga* is situated at the beginning of this trepidation driven road which is looked after by the Border Road Organization. All the vehicles halt here briefly for praying safe journey ritualistically. While most of the deep gorges across river Sutlej lead to beautiful valleys, this spine chilling precipice is horrendous, yet considered as the pride of Kinnaur by local folk.

I remember, during my childhood it was considered no child's play to venture towards tribal region, for the terrain was perilous, hallmarked by *Taranda Dhank*. Many laborers sacrificed their lives while opening this section of road through steep, one piece rock, rising almost to more than 90 degree angle up to 800 meters in one go from the base of river Sutlej.

In the year 2008 when we planned a journey up to *Kaza* (Spiti) with friends, I still remember the way we were ecstatic to have a view of this much talked *dhank*. We were not dejected. From the window of bus, all we saw was river Sutlej, roaring savagely with muddy water of monsoon rain over rock strewn bed.

One do always wonder, while having a look over these steep walls of single piece rock, without a crack in between, about the diligent work done in that era. It is truly marvel in terms of human determination.

On my second entourage to *Nigulsari*; a small town near *Taranda Dhank*, we visited the temple and clicked those mandatory *selfies*, which kept me wondering all the time, if I could traverse it one day.

As luck would have it, I got posted at *Nigulsari* in the year 2018. By this time I had developed trekking as my favorite hobby. I had travelled through many passes, seen different terrains. But scared I was to the extent with this steep *dhank* that I rarely ventured out towards this direction on routine basis, be it morning jog or otherwise, for I felt that the risk of a falling rock was high towards this side. So my routine jogs were rather towards opposite direction, a bit less risky, only on comparison basis though, for the whole of the tribal region is prone to rolling stones & rock fall.

It was only in the year 2020 when corona COVID 19 scare and complete lockdown kept everyone reclusive at one's own place. I also abjured to take the routine morning jogs towards *Nigulsari* bazaar as it might be infected with the abominable virus. Instead I preferred the peril of a falling rock at *Taranda Dhank*. Initially I would concentrate only upon the tarred road, rather than looking up at precariously dangling boulders. The narrow deep gorge just beyond *Taranda Mata* temple was so much steep that I would feel giddy, if I kept looking at it attentively. It was really shuddering.

After routine jogs and constantly appraising the gorge, one morning I decided to give it a try. I would clamber up to the last accessible point or maybe I find some approachable route up above the creek towards *Taranda* village, I thought.

As I moved up carefully, negotiating the dangerous scree, all I concerned about was the presence of any other human being on the highway below; looking up ghastly at my foolish act. Fortunately, this part of National Highway is rarely treaded by any person on foot except seasonal shepherds. I was accompanied by one local *Gaddi* dog of neighborer, who used to accompany me on morning jogs; I named it *Jhabru*, lovingly.

As he ascended the gorge carefully, I followed him slowly with mutual trust and motivation. Finally we were at the mouth of this *nullah*, the last accessible point; above which wild up rush of giant crags were biting into slow pacing clouds. A small trickle cascade through not-to-be-seen source up above. I rested there for a few moments. The highway lies far below us, only a small part visible with intermittent traffic. I was exalted with this task to the extent that I felt as if I was a part of this terrain as a whole. My spirits were high and my fears were gone. Now I was looking for some more challenging task of exploring the creek through another side.

I visited the village above this rocky terrain, beautiful *Taranda* valley, and found that through old Indo-Tibet road, there was some trail down towards National Highway, now rarely treaded. It became my obsession to decipher this trail and feel that adrenaline rush while traversing the mighty *Taranda Dhank.*

I surveyed the terrain again. A different route past *Dhank* was found, which must open up to less steep gully than the one I ascended previously with my canine friend.

I summoned my younger brother to bring one climbing helmet from Chandigarh, so that it may provide the much needed protection during proposed assault.

I brought my family along this summer, for the online classes of kid could be managed from any place and that hectic construction work back at *Duttnagar (Rampur Bushahar)* was over. I would relish the joy of living a family life after a long time. But, then I had become an acetic lampoon for long. I could not satiate my cravings for exploring the great *Dhank* and one morning I was negotiating the bushy terrain towards *Taranda* village on a reconnaissance.

This time I was accompanied by two canine friends, but at times they looked more like foes, for they would run frantically up above, oblivious about small pebbles being pushed down; which come rolling with extreme force from such steep heights. Keeping my foot carefully one ahead of another, avoiding swampy area across a small brook,

I reached up to the base of a steep cliff measuring almost 15 meters high. Although it was serrated intermittently, but one needed to be utmost wary and use the whole body to climb it up. I wished I had a rope. I gave it a try but soon thought that it won't be possible to creep down if I couldn't find any trail or approachable route ahead. Adrenaline rush with thumping heart was clearly appreciable. I gave up instantly and was soon sliding down the narrow rough funnel of that cliff. All the reveries of ascending above *Taranda Dhank* were deflated hence forth.

After few days that animal spirit flickered again, and I was looking for another route past swampy area, near middle of the cliff. I was in a quandary regarding timings of making the final assault. I thought I will do it after sending family back home, for I would be mentally relieved a bit, but then again I thought it would be awesome to enjoy a lavish homemade breakfast by my better half, after conquering the cliff. Also in any exigency they would raise the alarm if some untoward thing happens. I had revealed my plan of traversing the cliff to her in the past, but now she was much reluctant about my eccentric activities. She rather hoped that I somehow change my mind, for it was only me, who could stop myself from doing such things.

Then one day I suddenly found my trusted trekking shoes missing. On repeated enquiry it was found that she kept it back at home, for in its absence my climbing plans may get hindered as per her lame convictions!

Sunday early morning would be the day, and I would utilize all the available climbing gears, I thought.

Two days after my last *rekkie*, on dated 30.04.2021, I felt like going up again and explore the options across the swamp, while I was on my routine jog past temple. I was wearing the worn out running shoes, old tattered trousers, a big camouflage round army hat and a skipping rope in my pocket. Next two hours would be filled with extreme thrill and adrenaline rush, little did I know.

I bet; if anyone wants to relish the joy of being alive, do join me some day on this route. Adrenaline would rather ooze. For, it is primarily because of the appearance of this menacing mammoth cliff which obviously instills the natural fear merely by having a glimpse over it. To clamber over it is well beyond one's comprehension.

It was a routine working day. No proper gears were on, in fact I never thought about accomplishing it on this day only. Cold winds were pummeling my tardy face. I kept an eye over the passerby on the highway which fortunately was none. This time I clambered through the marshy slope, adjoining small brook, holding the thin vegetation growing over it. It was a pretty quick ascent. I never found difficulty up to last point, just beneath that proposed ledge where I had planned to land upon. Here it was again a big steep, crack-free boulder, to be climbed. I tried my best but again, thoughts of climbing it down if I somehow could not proceed further, sent shivers down my spine. I immediately turned back. I was about to declare it as an inaccessible path, but just then I found a small gap through the bushy thickets over the brook.

Surprisingly, here I found a kind of natural bridge over to another cliff, which seems less ominous. I made my way through it and climbed the boulder carefully. Soon I was on the top and guess; I was at the threshold of that small ledge, which would eventually lead me over to mighty *Taranda Dhank.*

Thereafter I found a small trail across the ledge, salutes to human ambitions, for it might have been traced well back centuries, although I was shuddering merely because of the thought of coming back through this route, if I could not reach the top. The narrow trail was my only hope as I saw livestock scrapping over it, intermittently. 'If animal could make it, so could I'; I convinced myself.

I concentrated only over the trail, for the slopes below were too steep and one would only feel giddy while looking downward and who knows a little slip would lead all the way down into river Sutlej almost 500 meters vertically below, with no chance of any stoppage in between. And last 200 meters would be air borne I knew, given the degree of inclination. My heart sank and I could feel that adrenaline rush again.

Soon the trail opened up to small, less graded open space. Scattered half burnt firewood were the signs that it was inhabited in recent past. I could feel the serene, chilling early morning blows, heard the screeching sounds made by three lammergeyers gliding atop the precipice and some rustling in the bushes.

Now the only worry was what if some wildlife inhabits this area? And my sudden presence would certainly alarm them, which may react impromptu. I started to cough violently. I even thought about wielding a piece of thick log, but then laughed on this foolish act. I would be defenseless and any encounter would be fatal for sure. I remembered God and my family. Poor guys don't even know that I was traversing the dangerous most cliffs. I found a small, used cartridge just below the trail, which was surely fired for the game. I had seen a few *gorals* (Nemorrhidus spp.) ambling atop the cliffs occasionally on my routine morning jogs. It surely was a good grazing area for them, but then rapaciousness of human beings doesn't spare them here too. Who knows some hunters were lurking around and misunderstood me for a prey! I was coughing again, involuntarily.

Till now the trail seems negotiable. I was of the opinion that I would tread the path only up to the point where I feel safe enough to get back. There was no point in ascending rough terrain only to find a dead end or a deep gorge and then returning back would be a challenge.

The place was serenely pristine and so was the trail. At one point I sat down beneath a big *deodar* tree and took a deep breath. I wish I could stay here for long, but sun had arisen and the day was getting hot.

Soon the trail came to a dead end unexpectedly. Sharp abrupt slope into deep gorge curtailed the path briskly. My goodness, I had to turn back, I thought. Just then I saw a small old fir tree fallen on one corner of a steep cliff. Beside that tree, I could appreciate a narrow passage leading to a small, man-made, stone-carved stairs; precariously leading up the cliff. It was a kind of Hillary's step with fixed ladders on Mount Everest! An exasperated analogy, but I apprehended the adrenaline rush for sure.

I followed it and admired human artisan qualities, which were visible at such terrain, where no one could have imagined a negotiable path through huge boulders. Just above that cliff, a broad plateau came to view with a few rhododendron trees blossomed at its best. What a mesmerizing view it was, Incredible!

Alas! I wasn't carrying any camera or cell phone to shoot the ethereal vista, but all I possessed was the lenses of my naked eyes.

Fragrance of wild jasmine flowers was so intense that I felt as if I were into heaven. I sat there for a few minutes and was in a kind of trance. I could see deep gorge down my left with a small patch of highway well below.

Although it was a cold windy weather, my body was drenched with salty sweat. The crispy wind pummeled my body soothingly and I was completely relieved. The way I had contemplated the height of *Taranda* village from National Highway was much higher than my expectations. I used to think that once I negotiate those rocky cliffs through the funnel shaped *nullah*, which I named *House's chimney*, past temple, I would reach the village in no time. How myopic we are while adjudging the things from below!

Once I reached the top of this gorge, I found that the actual height of the village was almost three times than I had contemplated.

Altitude enhances our view of life and we may appreciate how menial our approach or thoughts are.

After a few moments of introspection, I heard a few acquainted sounds. Human voices? I don't know why but

I never wanted any Homo sapiens around. Hunters? I got up quickly and took defensive position.

Adrenaline Rush.

Slowly I sneaked through the deep pit covered with thorny bushes and crawled towards the direction of intermittent sounds. I could appreciate three very minuscule figures, most probably some passerby, sitting up in the old Indo-Tibetan Road. May be they have spotted me ascending through the long forgotten trail or maybe they were just casually talking with each other. I was relieved at least there were no hunters around.

As I moved up through the narrow switchback trail edging the gorge, it also got disappeared after sometime. Where in the hell had it gone, that also after coming so far? I never wanted to turn back. I explored around and found a small green *bugyal* to the east, sizing around a small volleyball court and some apple orchards beyond the precipice. I must be just beneath the *dogri* of *Taranda* villagers. But, to negotiate this precipice through some unknown route might prove disastrous, I thought. Rather I decided to ransack the trail, for it must be lying around, how come it get disappeared so abruptly that also this far. Eventually, I succeeded.

As I meandered across the narrow edge of deep gully, keeping the foot cautiously, one behind another, I saw that big tower hallmarking the *Taranda* valley and the steel cable span ten meters above me.

Kudos, I made it!

I literally lunged to reach the final spot. What an incredible view. I could see *Taranda* village up above and the starting point of my today's much coveted journey. The National Highway swirls like a wane miniscule reptile and traffic like tiny ants.

At the top, wind was calm and refreshing. No human beings were around, though I could see some hovels dotting the apple orchards. The bridle path to *Taranda* village was clearly visible twenty meters ahead. I recognized it instantly for I had treaded it many times. I sat quietly there at least for five minutes and a strange kind of feeling swathed me all the time. I made it all alone, without any gear.

It was time to move, finally. Family members must have been waiting back at home. Just after taking a few steps forward, a ray of thought again popped up in my mind. I can always travel through this well known path; but I may never find enough time to get down by traversing the *Taranda Dhank*. Though I knew getting down safely is always much more difficult than ascending in this terrain, but the risk was worth taking. When shall I encounter this adrenaline rush again?

I turned back involuntarily.

The back journey was more enjoyable, for the sense of accomplishment has exalted the spirits. I was more cautious, for my shoes were worn out and the soles have turned flat. The dry needles of pine prove perfect recipe to get slipped. And here a slight slip means tumbling all the way down to river Sutlej 800-1000 meters vertically below. People describe *Rhogi*, near *Kalpa* (Kinnaur), as the suicide point, but to me *Taranda Dhank* is much earnest than that.

I negotiated the small narrow stairway with the help of my all limbs and was humming gaily while climbing down the narrow ledge. I sat below one old conifer tree whose bark was charred with brazen forest fire, but still its needles were growing green. Spirit of being alive; was motivational, despite all odds.

Now my only worry was to successfully descend through marshy creek. I was hoping that I still remember the path accurately, for if somehow I forget the way back, I had to pay a big price. Luckily I reached the small boulder and recognized it immediately. Below, I could see the terrain I followed past small brook flowing gallantly. I made a small stone cairn, for it may act as a landmark for the maverick travelers; if any. Passage through the marshy bushes and thorns was a little difficult but the spirits were high. I witnessed some stones rolling down ferociously all the way to highway, which were let loose by my body movements. How dangerous rather life threatening these small pebbles may turn, once they fall from such heights, with speed not less than a bullet. I realized the importance of a helmet.

And there I stood tall, on the highway, single piece, assessing the day's successful task. I did it man; all alone, I reassured myself. And then that involuntary jog towards *Taranda* temple started. The giant shuddering precipice of *Taranda Dhank* seems less terrible now, for I was traversing through its beautiful trail a few moments ago. In fact it wasn't me, but some other individual of my species, which has carved the way through this inaccessible nature's creation, in ultimate harmony.

Now all my wishes of conquering the cliff was over and it was a perfect aperitif for upcoming more serious summer expeditions. Relinquishing this material world while perusing the passion would be more meaningful than succumbing to some dreaded disease, I thought.

I reached back at home a bit late that morning; obviously the family members were anxious. All their thoughts turned true when I told them about my successful exploration exuberantly. But, over the time, especially my wife, had learned to keep equanimous, for her pleas are of no meaning, in the end! I told her that my expeditions at this place were over now, a bit considerate to her, I guess!

Hot water was already waiting in the washroom. While scrubbing my body, I whined casually, for the bruises encountered were painful. But then I laughed loudly, for the ecstatic pains of these bruises were more blissful than love bites…

Kinnaur Top to Sarahan Top

After spending quality time with family for a while, I felt as if I was still at unease due to lack of any preparatory trekking session before our final haul toward much coveted *Bhaba-Pin – Parvati* pass, scheduled for second fortnight of July could start. Though morning stretch-up session was not a routine; I tried my best to adhere with it as consistently as possible. Lately I had put some weight, thanks to my better half for sumptuous timely meals or may be due to stress free life. As my minimum tenure for serving in tribal region was already over, chances were rife that I might get transferred from this place. So, in order to maximize my explorations in this region a rough plan was expected to be contrived soon. Also towards the last week of June my trips back to home and *Shimla* for official and personal affairs kept me busy and I was unable to outline any upcoming hiking itinerary.

Also a complaint was lodged in the highest grievance redressal platform about not receiving any help regarding ailing animal due to shortage of staff. It needed to be carefully dealt with. So a late night visit was scheduled up to far flung *Rupi* (Kinnaur) area and matter resolved amicably next day at district head quarters *Rekong Peo.*

I was swathed with too much mental pressure and the only hope to relieve it was a detour up alpine pasture.

Fortunately I got a distress call from some shepherds tending their flocks up in *Tirmi Dhar* pasture atop *Taranda* valley, for their livestock was not all well. I chalked out a quick tentative schedule and mailed it to my old hiking partners Vijesh Guruji and local guy Vipin Negi. We would traverse towards *Sarahan* top, called *Bashal Kanda,* once done with treatment work. It was a short notice as the journey was about to commence within next two days. Obsessed I am with these mountains to the extent that I was resolute to move up all alone, if the two guys couldn't make it. As far as the weather forecast was concerned, I gave it a little head, for I am of opinion that the Almighty had created us with hard muscle and bones that we don't melt away in rain! Quite eccentric, Isn't it?

After initial hitches from Guruji's side regarding itinerary, I insisted for original schedule, to which he agreed eventually. After all, a call of the mountains is difficult to be ignored. Vipin told that he has got some urgent work at home and would reveal his decision on the eve of final journey.

I had to attend a marriage ceremony back at home the day before and rode back next morning to *Nigulsari*, my head still banging with late night binge.

After reaching my office, I concluded my official work and in extreme lethargy procured all the provisions needed for this sojourn. Off late I had purchased a small 1.5 liters Pressure cooker which would serve the purpose of cooking meals at high altitude. That evening my colleague from

Nichar, Dr Aasheesh joined me for some official work and of course with a pint of chilled beer. Amid scorching blows of summer air we relished the short rendezvous with chilled brew. By the time Guruji reached my place I was a bit teetering and over-conscious about final arrangements to be made.

Tirmi Dhar had already been hiked by me last summer but this time we were to explore inner valleys. Our journey would circumnavigate the *Bashal* top of *Sarahan* region. Two shepherds were ready to haul our luggage mid way as they were about to lead their pack animals with ration towards *Tirmi* base. It would have been a boon to any traveler for their loads would be carried over all the way to base camp, but to me it was all about endurance and preparation for upcoming big expedition up *Bhaba – Pin –Parvati* valley.

By dusk we had already procured and packed our rucksack with ration and provisions.

As we sat inside a small shop in *Nigulsari* Bazar enjoying evening drinks, another local guy and shop owner Mr. Anuraj Bisht, a relative of Guruji, showed his eagerness to join us. I second the thoughts of Vijesh that three are always better than two. All we needed to do was to replace *two men tent* with a *three men plus tent* lying at my office. As far as ration and provisions were concerned, we had packed sufficient to thrive for three days even when a grand reception was expected from shepherd's side. Vipin communicated late night that he won't be able to make it and we may proceed next morning as planned.

When I got up at 4.00 am to the alarm bell, I noticed overcast sky with mild drizzle. Should we defer the assault? I was in a quandary. By the time I prepared stuffed *Parathas*, Guruji was up and he professed that it would be mild rain, which would quell with passing day. I had no doubts to his predictions for the ecstasy of being up in the valley was so strong that we believed all fallacies.

Scheduled departure was at 5 AM, but as we kept an eye on weather, it was 6 AM when we moved finally. Anuraj's car hauled us up to last motor able point, *Chhonda* and only after puffing magic sticks we begin the hike. Mild drizzle still continued and we put on the rain coats. As we ascended the jungle trail up to *Kutangya*, sky cleared up and we soon found the sun smiling over the horizon.

At *Kutangya*, where small hovels of shepherds are dotted amid sylvan beauty, we met the young shepherds and had lavish breakfast of stuffed *paratha* and *dahi*. They insisted for putting our luggage on horseback but the only thing that I offered to them was our *three men tent* weighing 3 Kg and 700 grams. As of now I was feeling comfortable even with this tent on my back. Mountains of the mind are much tougher than actual one.

Slowly we switch backed through beautiful conifer forest. The trail was well known and within no time we were above tree line.

'Hirmu de' is a small knoll from where we can appreciate the beauty of *Bari* village, sprawling magnificently towards the other side of *Sholding Khad.*

The glade ahead is dotted with myriad colors of flower and the *Tirmi* top embellish with streaks of white glaciers.

The mist was swirling up the valley as sun thawed the cold frozen land. We captured this ethereal view in our cameras. Two young kids also accompanied us up to *Tirmi* base for they were equally excited to stay for that night with their relative shepherds. I wonder how tough these young chaps are, living an austere life since childhood, shepherds in making!

We were carrying a few bottles of local distillate, for the only thing that is in demand at such heights is the local booze. Also as per local belief, a *pooja* of reigning deity mandate bestowing the *Moori*, at every sacred place. We were offered *Chalamat* (to hold the distillate in folded palms) at all such places en-route, may be 4-5 times, so by the time we reachedbase camp, we were inebriated.

News of our arrival had already sneaked to the camp, so a grand feast was being organized for supper. We pitched our tent just next to shepherd's camp. It was 2 PM. We could have ascended further till the base of *Tirmi* top, but as our hosts were excited to shower their hospitality, we decided to stay here only.

A sumptuous lunch of Mix *Dal, Rice, curry* with local goat butter and *lassi* was served. We gobbled the feast while discussing various bliss and constrains of shepherd's life.

After resting for a couple of hours we explored the *bugyal* around. We were away from hustle and bustle of social life and the best thing was the absence of mobile signals. As we collected some firewood with shepherds, the drizzle started again. A beautiful rainbow scarffed the valley westward. It was an incredible view, my first rainbow of this monsoon! Soon the dissolutery rain led to swirling mist.

Vijesh was capturing every moment in his camera, off late he has become an amateur shutterbug. After collecting firewood we found shepherds mixing salt with cedar wood oil. On enquiring we were told that it is a traditional method to feed this salt mixed cedar oil to livestock as it quells many maladies. One shepherd told us that he even uses this therapy for himself intermittently, to keep the diseases at bay! A point of thorough research indeed!

We lay down under the clear sky relaxing as the dusk was setting in. Meanwhile a buck had been selected by the shepherds to be sacrificed that night. I examined the flock for any ailment; all were healthy barring a few suffering from foot Rot. We inoculated the medicines and distributed many to be applied later on. Shepherds were very happy. After ritualistic *pooja*, the buck was put to cleaver and soon the de-skinning work was in progress. How deftly these guys perform this business, as in no time palatable meat was ready to be cooked in the pan. A big conflagration was made and we again were taking *Chalamat*, this time with offals. Temperature plummeted with night as snowy peaks changed from white to amber gold. Big thanks to local potion and the bonfire that we enjoyed the feast before finally cuddling inside our coy, sleeping bags thus retiring for the day.

Young kids were so much ecstatic about our tent that they kept on leaping inside. One of the boys slept with us that night. Shepherds were equally enthusiastic and they requested me to order one big tent for them! I wonder why these nomads do not take full advantage of latest technologies rather than dwelling the traditional hardships.

After a sound sleep, I got up around 5 AM in the morning. Sky was pretty clear. Clouds were stationary in lower valley queued in a single row. Early birds were singing melodiously.

Horses and mules were grazing down hills, sheep and goat flocks relaxing calmly munching cuds beside our small camp. A shepherd was preparing morning tea.

Soon the other expedition members got up and after relishing nutritious goat-milk tea it was time to break the camp.

Today we would reach to the Top of *Tirmi Dhar* and explore the deep valleys.

The magnanimous shepherds bade us adieu only after gifting a small quantity of chevon for tonight's feast. We took mandatory selfie and hauled our luggage all the way up *Tirmi Dhar.* The weight of my rucksack has only increased with the addition of 3.7 Kg *three men tent.*

After hiking a gradual slope for almost an hour, we reached the base of *Tirmi* Top. I contemplated to traverse a bit eastward from where we could attempt a light assault to the top, but Vijesh was of the opinion to pitch the tent here only as the availability of water was plenty from nearby glacial stream and we need not to carry our loads further unnecessarily, for the way back towards *Bashal Kanda* lies through this trail. We all agreed instantly. This was the belvedere where we had pitched our tent last year with Vipin Negi, a beautiful knoll with glacial fed streams to the either side, though much lower than we had planned. It was near to the steep tongue of a minor glacier. My brand new Kerosene stove was put to use immediately. After fiddling for a few minutes, Vijesh was able to chug and pump it to maximum flame, which led to quick tea preparation. We savored it quietly and even filled our thermos, to be consumed later on the top.

At 8.30 AM we started the final light assault. I put a few eatables in my small reserve backpack with warm clothes and gloves. The sun was glittering marvelously in cloud free sky, but the fog was elevating gradually from the lower valleys as the day progressed. My previous experience reminded us that we have to be on the top as early as possible, for the mist may shroud the aura permanently as it happened with us last year and we had to wait for almost four hours on the top to let it settle, revealing sylvan beauty and cascading mountain ranges down.

At around 10 AM we reached the *Tirmi* top, a familiar terrain, but this time there was no glacier.

We appreciated the blissful view of *Rampur* valleys to the west, high glistening *Shrikhand* ranges towards the North, *Nichar* valley (*Kundi* Top) towards the East, and a huge mountain with loads of glaciers, *Belnu* top towards the south east. Farther up the south, colossal sky scrapping peaks towards *Sangla-Rohru* valley were mesmerizing.

As we captured the beautiful landscape in our gadgets, the wafting fog shrouded the view intermittently. Wind was soothingly crisp and the glade was dotted with myriad colored flowers. We rested for almost an hour on the top and then decided to explore the ridge towards big mountain southward. Vijesh was also eager to reach as much nearer as possible to the base of this huge mountain, while Anuraj followed lackadaisically.

We paced towards the far off small ridge laden with glacial ice. It seemed as if we would be able to reach there in no time but the big boulders carried down by the old glaciers, hindered our pace and at one place we sat down panting vigorously. Altitude was conjuring its effects.

It was time to repose and replenish our energy and what else could have been more refreshing than a cup of hot *Masala* tea and brown breads laced with apple jam! The shot of energy was instant. Fiddlehead fronds pickle brought by Anuraj was the perfect ending to this small alpine feast.

After a brief rest we started our hike again traversing the scree and negotiating the morains intermittently. Meanwhile, these big mountain ranges were playing hide and seek as the mist was culminating in large quantity.

As we reached the western end of glacial ridge, we found abrupt abyss to the other side. Nothing was visible due to constant fog. All we could do was to wait and take rest. We must have rested for a couple of hours in vain as there was no sign of weather clearing up. I decided to move a bit upward, maybe I could find something but again the ridge dropped to unknown chasm to this side as well.

All I could hear were rocks falling constantly which must be big breaking glaciers or huge crags.

Belnu Top altogether is a splendid scene of mountain savagery and frigid beauty. It is called *Jomparing (*way to hell) in local dialect for the incessant rock fall emanates loud trepidating noises all the time from this shrouded mountain range. It is believed that only the spirits of dead people move past these mountains, where no one has dared to venture in life time!

There was no sign of weather clearing up and the clock had struck 3PM. Moreover some ominous dark cumulous were developing west ward. Soon the thundering and lightening began and as expected it started to drizzle which further exacerbated to a fully fledged hail storm. While we skidded off through small glacier, the terrain up above had turned silvery white.

Suddenly the fog cleared and a magnificent view of Belnu top was evident. Huge glittering glaciers were present on the mountain and at very first instance it seems inaccessible. However a shoulder dropped south ward with the hope of some distant pass towards *Rohru-Chirgaon* region. We wished that we could wait for some time and try to explore a bit deeper, but then the intensity of storm increased and the only option that we were left with was to head back towards base camp as soon as possible.

Thundering and lightening was so much frightening that we were forced to take shelter in a small cave.

Temperature dipped significantly and the bare hands were trembling with cold. I put my gloves on and the wind cheater served the purpose. The thundering was echoing through the high peaks and candidly I hadn't heard such loud and prolonged thunder in one go.

We waited for this storm to quell which mellowed down only after an hour.

As we progressed back to base camp we found a flock of local *Rampur Bushari* Sheep. The known shepherd invited us to their tarpaulin covered temporary shed and exchanged pleasantries. They were about to prepare a tea but then it would take some time to burn wet twigs. The location of this camp was so beautiful that we could see the snowy peaks eastward and deep lush green valley northward. *Gaddi* dogs were wary about our every movement. We saw a mesmerizing rainbow across the valley and giant silvery ranges in the backdrop. I offered the shepherds some medicines and examined their huge cache of reserve drugs. This is general habit of the shepherds to collect medicines from wherever they could; before proceeding to alpine pasture, for the fear of any outbreak at such remote region would surely devastate their livelihood. However most of the medicines get expired without any use.

After a brief halt we proceeded toward base camp. *En route* just above the camp site we collected dry twigs of dwarf rhododendron the only firewood we could get here. Sky was still cloudy but the rain had stopped.

While I and Vijesh arranged the cooking material, Anuraj made a small fire, despite mild drizzle. Under the shade of umbrella, previous night's sacrificed goat meat was sauté in small pressure cooker. In the meantime the first pour of our last cache of local distillate was offered to *Pooja* and we took the first *chalamat* of the day. Small disposable glasses had worn off and the only way to gulp it down was after holding it in *cul de sac* palms. With the first shot of potion, a queer headache developed. I was not in a mood to take medicine, but kept pondering how come it happened even at lower altitude? Earlier I felt all fresh and rejuvenated at *Tirmi* Top. But anything may happen on such heights. Anuraj suggested a local panacea and soon he was rolling a *tendu* leaf filled with high quality wild cannabis. Candidly, my experience with the weed is not encouragingly blissful, for it develops some psychological issues after being consumed, but as of now it seems the pretty deal. It was encircled among us, and the most excited was Vijesh. Headache slowly mellowed.

No sign of any wind was appreciated. Air was still. After dark the sky cleared suddenly, revealing a star lit expanse, glaciers and the dim form of peaks beyond it. We danced, yodeled and whistled over the local songs, thanks Guruji for small bluetooth speaker. We enjoyed the perfectly cooked chevon, courtesy mini pressure cooker. While Vijesh and Anurag enjoyed late night, post-supper gossips, I slipped inside my sleeping bag, for the headache had suddenly picked up.

I got up to uneasy smothering apprehension in middle of the night around 12.30 AM. Headache was gone but so was the comfort. I lie awake, marveling at my folly for voluntarily exchanging the comfort of civilization for the discomfort of the high mountains.

Wind has picked up and the thin walls of our tent were fluttering tumultuously. I felt like staying awake. After almost an hour I again fell fast asleep, only to get up late in the morning.

It was a calm and blissful morning. As we strolled through the glade we saw unique strata of clouds pervading lower valleys. Surreal view it was in fact. We again made a fire and prepared breakfast of *Maggi*, bread and tea. We were to traverse the *Bashal Kanda* and circumnavigate the *Sarahan* valley.

At around 8.30 we finally broke the camp. Packing and decamping require hell a lot of time, indeed.

The route up to *Sirkund* top *via Fulyari Dhar* was well known to me, for I had trod it last summer with Vipin Negi.

At *Fulyari Dhar* we met another shepherd, who was in search of medicines for his ailing flock, and guess I was looking for the same for I was still carrying some loads of medicines in my backpack and wanted to unload it before we move to *Bashal* top. The shepherd told us that he had been to *Belnu Kanda* (*Pishting*) many years ago and was privy to those strange sounds. He even confirmed the presence of some precious stones on that mystical mountain.

At *Sirkund* top, we rested for tea. We had covered almost half the distance presumably and it was just eleven in the morning. I was well aware about the fact that by noon, the swirling fog would shroud the valley and we may astray from actual route. Though we outlined the trail roughly from top, but as we followed it later, we felt lost. We were descending much steep and abruptly than expected. It must not be the way towards *Bashal.* Vijesh was sent for a *rekkie*, but soon came back unconfirmed. Had it not been that small fraction of seconds when fog cleared momentarily and we could see small hovels of *Kinnu* valley, just opposite to *Sarahan* valley, the only option would have been but to descend the treacherous rocky terrain to the other side of our destination. For we had arranged transport at *Sarahan* town, we ought to reach near it.

Hauling our heavy luggage back up the valley literally lunging, we soon corrected our course and were near the ridge through which bridled path led us all the way to *Bashal.* We met some gujjar nomads who confirmed that we were on right path. Hereupon journey was all new to me, for we had traversed down through *Sirkund* Lake last year, circumventing *Bashal.*

The pony trail was wide enough insinuating that it had been trod since time immemorial. Tree line was much below our path. We found *primulas*, *aconitum* and a few *prime roses* en route, though the number was lesser than *Tirmi* top where the green carpet beholds numerous colored flowers, difficult to prevent its sorrowful trampling. But here many more species of flowers were yet to bloom.

We reached to a broad balcony of a ridge from where we had a magnificent view of entire 15/20 valley (archaic name) of *Rampur riyasat*, towards the right flank of river Sutlej, intersected by many small brooks and rivulets. Vijesh guruji was more than happy to locate his village and neighboring area. We had a fare view of far *Shrikhand* ranges. Vijesh's spirit was exalted with the thought that he would proudly point his finger towards *Bashal* from his home at *Ganvi* village, while sipping a cup of tea on a chilly winter morning when the terrain will be painted white and would tell his kids that he had inched every corner of this mountain.

We took some concluding photographs here, for the fog again started to rise. I took off my snow goggles and round army hat, to pose for some memorable portrait. In the hush-hush of proceeding further, I never knew that I had forgotten to pickup my snow goggles. Only at the lower deeper jungle of *Bashal*, did I apprehend that I had made a mistake but then to comeback from that far, just to pick up a material thing was well beyond my resolution. I was rather happy that I was physically and mentally in perfect shape as of now.

From ridge, where we rested, the trail to *Bashal* looked short but as we trod gradually, it seems like never ending process. Those small hillocks kept erupting one after another. Our potable water was at the verge of exhaustion and we couldn't found any source of fresh water en route. Last source of water was just beneath *Sirkund* top, and we had walked for almost 4 hours since then. At one point we met some local guys tending to their livestock. They told us that now it was a downhill journey altogether and we may find some water source in the jungle.

As we descended along the sharp ridge, we reached thick moss laden *kharshu* (Quercus) jungle. We were told that this broad trail will lead us all the way to Sarahan.

As we followed the given trail, we progressed down to conifer forest. When did we astrayed from original path we never knew. It was Vijesh who apprised us about our mistake, by that time we had already swayed far away from *Sarahan* toward *Rangori* village, his in-laws.

Anuraj and Vijesh fiddled with *google* map with utmost confidence to find the actual route, but my hopes were miniscule, as I had been deceived by this app many a times, that also in urban areas, least to expect in thickets of bushy rugged terrain.

We rested on a cross trail wondering which way to go, one descending southward and another ascending in opposite direction.

I surveyed a trail heading upward, only to find that we were to ascend a steep terrain to oblivion with full baggage on our back. We must follow our basic instincts at such occasion. For safety one must rely over instincts rather than a reasoned knowledge of mountain-craft. There was no point in keep muscling up and we turned back abruptly, what if we reach to the far end of *Sarahan*. We can always call a cab that far. We were tired a lot and hungry as well, so we took the last sip of water before engulfing the lunch, raw. It was a grand luncheon of *paneer*, cucumbers, cashew, almonds, onion and tomatoes. There was no prudence in taking this last chunk of eatables all along home, for it was our last meal of the journey. We rationed the left out water and it was an awesome final feast indeed.

We still had enough ration to survive for one or two nights, thanks to the hospitality of shepherds, for even after strict allocation of daily ration we had plenty of it unused.

Dal, rice, *maggi*, dryfruits, jam, pickle and many other eatables ought to be carried back home. It's always bolstering to keep our stores replenished till end.

As we wandered through the thick forest of *Bashal* foothills, all we could do was to follow the broad bridled path downwards the valley, even when it was digressing westward completely opposite direction to *Sarahan*. Vijesh was now convinced that we must have reached towards his in-laws house at *Rangori* Village.

Sometimes exasperation makes the distance feel like eternal. We were not in a position to try any shortcuts as the fear of astraying further was mightier and it was four o'clock in the evening.

Just as we trudged down never ending forest canopy tacitly, a dog ran towards us wagging its tail. It was the only creature that we met almost for a past couple of hours. Either he must be accompanied by his master or we were near to human habitation.

As we were patting and cajoling the canine friend we saw a bearded man with a big hair lock embellished with a long wild bird feather, sitting over the ledge overlooking the lush green valley. He greeted us warmly and was more than happy to help us. His accent clearly pronounced that he was a denizen to this part of the world.

Arindam Aditya inhabits these pristine valleys for past more than two years. A former biology researcher, after post graduating from Kolkata he came for his research work in nearby *Sarahan* pheasantry. Fascinated he was to the extent with these placid picturesque deep valleys that he left his job and became a permanent wanderer seeking Nirvana at an early age. (He must be in mid twenties I guess). As I asked him quite obvious question about how he make his living, his answer was curt and determined, that his necessities are bare minimum to be met with his part time jobs, be it working for a local guest house as social media manager or to work as guide for solo travelers. He has taken hiking enthusiasts up to *Saat mai* Trek, past remotest *Kashapat* village in *Rampur* Tehsil, just beneath *Belnu Kanda,* that we were up to, yesterday; but to opposite side.

We all reposed here for some time putting down our rucksack. Vijesh asked him inquisitively that where did we diverted from actual path? He told that a little trail towards east direction just beneath the ridge must have been hidden under long bushes, would have taken us to *Sarahan.*

After resting for a brief period, he led us towards nearby motor able road. We chatted ecstatically while trailing the beautifully boulevard path.

Soon we reached to a small village *Ladowala*, to see first human inhabitation in past 3 days. Aaditya showed us the trail downwards. He also took us to a small slated traditional house, from where Vijesh collected potable water. I saw him gulping whole the bottle down his throat in one go. We also drank to our fill.

Aaditya insisted to lead us further down to road but we insisted back. I told him that he should treat his dog

Lalu for mange caused by mites and recommended some drugs to be administered at the earliest. He was highly obliged. We bid farewell and pounced back on the track, following *Lalu*. A motor able *kutcha* road lies further down in the valley. We passed two or three small hamlets on the way, all lacking modern sheen and grandeur all due to lack of road facilities. We were really astonished with the fact that *Sarahan Bushahar* had been a reigning capital of whole *Bushahar riyasat* for many centuries, but on the name of development not even a small ambulance pass way was constructed thus far? What kind of politics it was, we wondered.

At around 5.30 pm we finally touched the road. The cool wind of alpine pasture was replaced with humid, heavy gush as we perspired below our loads.

Car was waiting for us. It was time to take the final *selfie* before we threw up our luggage into the trunk of car and we're really spirited after successfully circumnavigating the whole stretch from *Sholding Nullah* Kinnaur to *Manglad Khad* Shimla district, without any untoward incident, in a single piece.

May be to others the journey was over but to me it was just an evaluation of my physical and mental endurance before a big expedition expected in coming days with old buddy Billu Wangpa.

We had not conquered the Mountains but to ourselves.

The Bharal Stories

I was born and brought up in a small village in the hill state of Himachal Pradesh. Since my childhood I have heard about constant conflicts between Human and wildlife. At times I also used to accompany my Mom and other village women for collecting forage from adjoining jungle. It used to be a harsh journey indeed, especially in summer season when the scorching sun would penetrate its rays through tanned skins of bowed back women, for it was lean season and scarcity of fodder was bound to happen. Occasionally a few encounters used to take place and we heard about man/women being attacked by a Himalayan bear which still continue today. But the *ghasani* (forest land marked for collecting forages) system was quite good in terms of preventing forest fire, for it was collective responsibility of villagers to ensure that their scarcity fodder doesn't burnt to a cinder.

In my adulthood professional obligations lead me to explore various places, passes and mountains in different parts of the state. Sometimes sporadic disease outbreak used to occur in far flung area of remote alpine pasture and a team of professional Vets would be summoned immediately to attend the same. For me, it was like blessing in disguise as it was an opportunity to explore the remotest parts of the state. In the mean time my propensity towards mountain climbing also developed. It was a routine to indulge in one or more mountain expedition every summer. Of late I got transferred to District Kinnaur. Snow clad mountains were more than *aperitif* for mountain climbing.

The first hiking that we took was *Bhaba-Pin* Pass. It is much commercialized trek treaded by many hikers throughout the summer up to late fall. We hiked it in the month of April 2018. I had already explored the trail up to *Karra* Lake previous year, when I was deputed with Animal Husbandry Department livestock at high alpine pasture. In the last week of May and first fortnight of June as much as seventy thousand sheep & goats enter the *Bhaba* Valley for grazing purpose, a lot many of them cross over to Spiti valley for almost three months. Chances of disease outbreak are inundate, for flocks arrive here from across many districts of the state. In the month of April, only a few hikers venture out through this trek as chances of glaciers on the way are too high.

The hike starts at small picturesque village of *Kafnu* where a Dam is built to store water for *Bhaba* Hydroelectric Project. *Bhaba* valley, which initially looks narrow; gradually widen as we hike through thick forests of *Gyaru* above *Homte* village. Pine trees gradually are replaced with fir and spruce. One can find thick Rhododendron, oak and Birch intermittently.

As we moved through idyllic meadows of *Mulling* we suddenly spotted some movements past big boulders & scree bordering the plain. The camouflage was so perfect that to distinguish anything was very difficult. As we stood amazed for a while, to our surprise we found a group of *bharal* (Himalayan Blue Sheep, *Pseudoisnayaur*) watching intently towards us. For the first time my eyes witnessed the beauty of this sturdy creature. Up to now we had only heard stories about *bharals* and snow leopards from local shepherds. But their presence during peak summer season, when human activities are at helm, is minuscule in this region.

Bharal or blue sheep has a mixture of sheep like and goat like traits. They have stocky body and stout legs with robust shoulders and broad chest. Their pilage ranges from grayish brown to slate brown, hence the common name Blue Sheep. Their hair is short and they lack beards. They are found in the high Himalayas of India, Nepal, Bhutan, Tibet, Myanmar and Pakistan. They live on high pasture slopes and usually found near rocky cliffs, and try to avoid forested areas. They are very much sure footed and traverse through barren, highly unstable precipices with utmost agility. These animals are tolerant of extreme weather conditions and can be found from dry hot desert mountains to windy cold snowy slopes. These are herbivores and usually thrive over high grassy slopes.

We captured a few photographs from a distance through our cell phones, for we were not carrying any professional photography equipments as we have never ever thought about finding any wildlife. For a while the group remained still, but then slowly started to criss-cross the steep perilous mountain with utmost agility until they dwindled with the brown shade of hercules mountain, beyond recognition.

The camouflage of their coat color with the surrounding environment, mostly high precipices, is so extreme that it's really difficult to distinguish if they remain motion less. Once they have been noticed however, they scamper up to precipitous cliffs, where they freeze again, and using camouflage to blend into rock face.

We rested for the night there itself, my dreams full of *bharals* all around our camp. We broke the camp early morning next day; with overcast weather and started to ascend immediately. By the time we reached *Karra* lake drops had turned into snowflakes. Aura had transformed magically white around. We waited for storm to quell underneath a big inclined boulder, but it only increased with time. So, we were forced to march down quickly, with tempest glee on our faces, for we had seen the coveted Himalayan Blue Sheep for the first time.

My second encounter with *Bharal*occurred after a few months. This time expedition was towards *Kunnu-Charang* Valley in Pooh block of District Kinnaur. This terrain is quite in contrast with Bhaba Valley. It is more kind of cold desert. Altitude wise *Bhaba-Pin Pass* stood at 4890 meters, while *Charang* Pass is about 5300 meters, *Bhaba* valley is sylvan whereas there is not much vegetation in *Kunnu-Charang* valley.

It was occasion of *Janamashthami* & as per local folklore; an ardent devotee of Lord Krishna should perform *parikrama* of kinnour Kailash holy mountain through *Charang La*. The hike started at small village *Charang* bordering Tibet (There is no mobile network here and only one satellite phone is provided by the Govt. to whole village). A renowned monastery *Rangrik Tungma* is situated at the outskirts of *Charang* village. Monks live here through all seasons. Our guide was a local fellow, incidentally our schoolmate and classmate. He explained everything about tough terrain & life in this remote village. Most of the people of this village follow Buddhism. Pea is the only cash crop here. People rear livestock, which are goaded to high alpine pasture in summer season. As per Chhewang Dorje, *Bharals* are in plenty here given the strong Buddhism influence, for compassion towards all living being is preached and practiced. There is no place for violence. When the numbers of prey are high, so are the predators. No wonder, at times one may hear the roars of Snow leopards echoing through barren rough mountains. Chhewang also told us interesting story *en route* about his wild voyages once he came back to his native place after completion of his formal education in a boarding school. Like any other teenager he was enthusiastic about going for a game, every weekend even when it was considered unholy and abominable by most of the villagers and heavy penalties were imposed if someone were caught doing so. Given the outside modern bringing up of Chhewang, he didn't give it a damn until that day. They chased the *bharal (Locally known as 'nabu')*flock for almost up to two days without any success, hungry and exhausted. Finally when target was achieved, the carcass rolled down all the way into deep gorge. A few of his friends turned back, but for him it was all about pride. They somehow managed to retrieve the carcass, after sheer hard work for another exhaustive day, only to be confronted by villagers including their family members who were waiting their arrival. Not only were they fined heavily but also ostracized from the society. Only after repeated vows, not to do such things in future, were they accepted by the society. Due to such stringent community based actions, wildlife thrives here in plenty. As we scaled up the *Charang* Valley we were shrouded by thick fog, reducing visibility to bare few meters. We also met a few army men, who were not on duty but had hiked all the way for three hours to get mobile connectivity. They seem happy to get connected with their family members and so were we!

As we descended through narrow perilous gorge the mist suddenly quelled and to our surprise a flock of seven *bharals* was ascending towards us. For the wind was blowing in opposite direction they could not smell us, walking carefree until the leader gauged the threat and leapt suddenly. After a while we saw another flock of eight *bharals* ambling uphill. We managed to take a few photographs with our inapt cell phones, but were happy to watch these graceful animals for the second time in this season.

Bharals are gregarious with group size ranging from five to four hundred individuals. The wide range of herd size depends upon season, population size, habitat condition, hunting pressure and disturbance. Herd composition changes frequently as any member of group may join or part. Poaching for meat, trophy kill and competition with other wild and domestic animals (overgrazing) pose a threat to them. Currently the species is classified as Least Concern (LC) on IUCN Red list.

We descended the gorge gleefully and took the path along clattering rivulet. For that evening we pitched our tent at *Lalanti* pasture. It is a broad bugyal dotted with various colorful flowers; Gentians, Primulas, Iris, Himalayan Blue Poppy, Himalayan aster etc. were in plenty. Forest department of Himachal has built a permanent shed here. Pilgrims & shepherds stay inside when needed but presently in dilapidated condition. Next morning our journey started at 5.00 AM only to be greeted by red billed choughs. At the base of *Charang* La, amid big boulders brought down by glacial moraines we found Juniper shrubs which are collected by local folk for incense. It took arduous climb of almost one and half an hour to reach the pass. *Chhitkul* valley embraces the other side with its own distinct flora & fauna.

Winter Climbs; Invincible Or Not

2021

Winters had always been an adventure trove to me atleast on literature front. I took the task of accomplishing a few adrenaline rush books, source of constant motivation for summer hiking.

'The long walk' by Slavomir Ravicz was just an awesome read, leave aside its veraciousness. 'Into the heart of Himalayas' by Jono Lineen is equally appreciable and inspiring one. One book which still lies over my bookshelf, wrapped in flimsy polythene cover, unscathed, is 'The valley of flowers' by Frank S Smythe. Wish I am done with it before the onset of the springs.

Last two winters were spent in infirmary, with mother's convalescence. There was no thought about keeping body fit and healthy for coming summer sojourns as mind was sickened for long. For she lost the battle eventually hence this winter was all about memories. Memories of worst phase; thriving in a messed up enclosure and memories of best phase of exalting in the pure thin air up in the Himalayas.

How could I forget the adrenaline flowing in my veins at its peak while crossing the gushing glacial, waist high stream in *Bhaba* valley? The way we were about to make a blunder by traversing the perilous rocky terrain late evening above *Tia* plains, that mid-night hike with burning barks of *Bhojpatra* in *Nichar* valley or those involuntary dancing stances with sole intoxication of beautiful landscapes around at *Tirmi* Top?

Though I scaled only a few peaks, vicariously, with these mountaineering books this winter, but the home affairs curtailed my expectations.

I met *Billu Wangpa*, my old hiking partner on a couple of occasions this winter, who was much enthusiastic about a winter expedition, be it for a short period. *"Ek tou banta hai, Sir".* (One must be there). I am not sure about myself, dwelling in my small inappropriate, cheap, tarpaulin tent, in extreme winters, but the thrill of camping amid white glistening snowy ambience would be once in a life time affair. So, I asked him to plan one expedition, before the springs, but as of now no communication received from his side.

I have carved my natural trekking season from early summers to early fall. For some it starts as late as early winters! I always wondered that, is it possible to scale high peaks in extreme season?

When I started to read literature on climbing, I was very much enthusiastic to know that if people are getting heady for summiting the highest peaks in summers, will there be some who would assault the same in extreme winters? For the limits of one's endurance would only be tested in worst conditions.

The beauty of a landscape gets only embellished in snowy silvery aura but its more than that, about sheer determination to prove one's strength, both physical and mental. The challenge of a winter climb is obviously more. The support staff is difficult to be arranged, which otherwise is easily available in routine summer season. Even administration is geared up in normal hiking season to deal with any eventuality, which of course is not expected in sheer winters in the absence of routine climbing activities.

Later, I learnt a few, if not many, seasoned mountaineers which had already accomplished the task of being on the top in those conditions, many perished in doing so. Anatoli Boukreev, a hero for some and a villain to others, never came back from Annapurna after winter expedition of 1997. Many experienced climbers lost their lives only to mingle with their beloved mountains, even when they knew the chances of weathering the storms up above were much less in extreme conditions.

All of the eight thousander fell to human ambition and determination in winters except the savage mountain K2, the world's second highest peak at 8611m (28251Ft) and also reputedly the deadliest one, where one out of every four climber, never make it back. Only five attempts to scale it in winters has been made since its first summer ascent in 1953, and all of them failed. It is a challenge, as always and there were almost five dozens of aspirants, inhabiting Baltoro glacier by late last year. Scaling K2 in winters was perhaps the last great prize of high altitude mountaineering. Mountain climbing enthusiasts were keeping an eye over the activities taking place there in winters of 2020.

Advancement of technology was keeping people updated about each and every move regarding any assault on the unconquered one. But such rush for summit push was unprecedented, and who knows a big tragedy was waiting ahead! I was skeptical. Especially in winters, to scale a peak, most dreaded even for summer assault, only experienced climbers dare to plan about it. But still whenever the number of aspirants increases so does the chances of a tragedy. I also kept myself updated about this K2 expedition by reading small blogs being fed over internet, intermittently.

And then the news came that ten Nepali nationals would try to accomplish the task in coming days. Nine Sherpa and one Magar, formed a team, off late, cutting across different expedition at the Godwin Austin Glacier in remote corner of Pakistan. Soon we saw what whole world celebrated with these brave mountaineers, singing Nepali National Anthem over the top of Savage Mountain, which eventually fell against human will and resolution. And most deserving to these indigenous mountain people who in all way assisted the westerns since the climbing affair began, on almost all expeditions. I watched over and over again the small clip of these guys ambling at the top of K2, instilling sheer ecstasy each time.

It was all about right planning, right composure, and exquisite team work and off course good luck. None of the team members were in a haste to reach at the top for making history. In fact all of them waited for each other a few meters below the summit and ascended to the top holding each other's arms. A touching moment indeed. Nation first.

Many climbers were to test their limits and meet their fate in coming days on K2, for the weather was mostly unfavorable leaving only a small window for final assault.

And then came the update about a team which would try for final summit push shortly. It included an Icelander John Snorri, Chilian Juan Pablo Mohr (JP) and two Pakistani father – son duos, the veteran Mohammed Ali Sadpara and his 21 year old son Sajid Ali sadpara. All were experienced climbers with many highest peaks under their belts. Constant newsfeeds were coming from K2 about their progress. The team would go for summit push on 5th February 2021, one of the news blog declared. It was snowing here, the first snowfall of this year and we all were enjoying the same. For a day or two I kept busy in home affairs and no newsfeed came from K2. Perhaps it would be second summiting of K2 this season and a routine thereafter!

After a couple of days news came that the base camp has lost contact with the climbers and the junior Ali is on his way back, for he experienced some health problems at the *bottleneck* and is descending down to base camp. By all possibilities the team should have been back on camp four, within 24 hours of their final assault. Young Sajid Ali waited for them at high camp but on constant pursuance headed down due to his personal bad condition.

A storm up the mountain would have forced the three men to bivouac for that night and must be back sooner. Whole world was waiting for that good news. As per Sajid Ali, they all were in good shape, when he turned back from bottleneck around 8000 meters height. All were experienced fellow and in fact at few occasions Ali Sadpara has narrated about making an ice cave and surviving the night, if the condition demanded so. The batteries of their satellite phone were dead hence couldn't be contacted. 48 hours, without contact.

I posted my comment on a *Facebook* page mentioning, "Miracle does happen sometimes. Wishing for a safe arrival. Brave work", to which one of the viewer wrote, "Its K2. At 8000 meters for 48 hours, No miracle happens."

Help for rescue poured from all across the globe. Pak Air Force helicopter, high altitude C130 aircraft, made various sorties in 2-3 days despite constantly bad weather, and used infrared technology to spot possible shelter on the peak. They flew upto 7800 meters with mountain experts and high resolution cameras. Even the base camp Sherpa of the expedition also accompanied one of the sorties, to help them locate the possible route, but no signs were found. Rescue operation was finally suspended nine days later, for the weather was constantly unfavorable. Two Pakistani Mountain climbing veterans and relatives of Sadpara tried to search the route upto *bottleneck* but without any success.

One of the blog declared, "A day long search and rescue mission to locate three missing mountaineers on K2 has been officially concluded with no sign of Mohammed

Ali Sadpara, JP Mohr and John Snorri. The mission included both aerial and on ground efforts using satellite images, last collected GPS Data of missing mountaineers and information provided by Sajid Ali Sadpara." (16.02.2021), a Pakistani official stated.

Perhaps miracle doesn't happen at 8000 meters, indeed. Rest in Peace was my next comment, a week later when the whole mountaineering fraternity was mourning the great loss. A strange kind of exasperation hallowed me, even when the lost souls were not acquainted to me in any way. They were there neither for claiming the first ascent, nor to prove anything to anybody. They were just living their passion even after knowing the grave perils of being at such heights that also in extreme weathers. And then the question rises again, "Why?"

Perhaps the same reply they must have given, "Because it is there."

Well, the spirits of these climbers must be free and at peace after mingling with the ice and rocks, they loved the most. Some people are already dead when they are so called, living; and a few live even after being physically gone.

The winters of 2020-21 would not only be remembered for successful ascent of K2, but for the loss of legendary mountaineers, that entire world mourned. Moreover people love to read and remember a tragedy rather than a routine success.

Well, I don't have any plans to venture out that extreme and is content with my contemplative summer slow expeditions upto low passes. As Jono Lineen rightly said, "…walking is what human beings were designed to do… the drop of a heel, the roll onto the ball of foot, the flex of toes and the push off with a bend of knee, is so embedded that that there is home deep within the movement." Also to me, walking up a hill is just like a meditation.

But then the danger of being on a mountain always remain same, be it an eight thousander or a five thousander.

Winters are almost at its end. Second fortnight of February is soothing in comparison to extreme winters. But this time it's more than that, for the winters was not that much colder and we witnessed meager snowfall only for a couple of times. That extremities numbing cold is no more appreciable now. Thermal wears were least used. That chilling gusts of morning blows; outside my spartan shanty is a thing of past. Myriad birds are chirping around, ready to welcome the impending springs. Vehicular traffic not that much regular over National Highway – 5 at early hours of the day. I resumed my routine morning jog since last week. It was rather a reconnaissance regarding early morning weather conditions, which I found just perfect, in consonance with joggers delight. Though early morning outdoor running activities were suspended due to cold winter conditions for past almost two months but the indoor calisthenics work was being performed uninterrupted. In fact morning jogs continued intermittently even at home *(Rampur,* HP*)*, for the climate was a bit warmer over there. I worked in my apple orchards and the much desired winter activities like pruning, training, application of fertilizers& manure, preparation of beds, planting new saplings, grafting old plants and application of pesticides were accomplished on time.

Sundays were always reserved for farm activities, you miss one and the work gets postpone for next 7 days or may be two weeks. It's a time bound process, straying from the recommended window may waiver the chance of a promising crop. So in this melee, when did winter passed, I never knew. Billu Wangpa's reply was still awaited.

I couldn't rejig my old memories when the whole family used to bask the sunday winter sun over terrace and enjoy usual badinage and banters over many rounds of tea, overlooking the snowy serrated peaks of *Shrikhand* ranges in the backdrop.

Professionally we were more focused about achieving targets, which to my mind were unrealistic. For the work assigned was much skewed to that of our professional expertise. It was rather an extension work that was being goaded incredulously.

Thoughts of any winter expedition were non-pragmatic as springs were just at threshold. All I wished summer sojourns would start early this year and hoped that corona scare would quell by that time.

I contemplated to explore Uttarakhand Himalayas and Dhauladhar ranges this season.

With the hope that readings of this winter would fillip the needed enthusiasm for seeking solace and self realization in upcoming sojourns, I saluted the departed soul, tacitly.

Twofer – I

In the year 2020, we decided to explore inner valleys of Bhaba, Kinnaur district. For it was Corona restrictions all around, local valleys were perfect place to venture into. With some of my colleagues who are also posted in nearby area, we unanimously planned to firstly scale well known *Bhaba-Pin Pass* and then to explore dreaded, less known *Bhaba-Lippa Pass*. This expedition was named as *Twofer*, for we were to top two high passes both above 5000 meters, in a span of more than a week. My diary excerpts during this twofer of ten days, is mentioned in this chapter.

STAGE 1: BHABA-PIN

14.08.2020 9.52 AM *NIGULSARI*

It rained thoroughly whole night. This morning, fog is all around, but sky a little bit clear. Now we expect a clear weather by noon. Everything is packed and is in order. I am waiting for Rajeshwar Negi, a localite and one of the members for this expedition. I need to buy a small pocket diary, for it is not advisable to carry a big routine alamnac. Everyone (hikers) seems to be pumped up. All those ecstasies to be in the wilderness are brewing up with each passing moment. I charged my batteries (mobile, head lamp, power bank, torch) all through night. Couldn't get a sound sleep last night for it was those strange excitements which are always expected before any expedition.

Now as we are already set to put our feet on trail leading all the way up high Himalayas, hardly does it matter if it rain or not. Preparations are replete for any bad weather up there, though it would be blissful jaunt if the sky clears. I talked to family, backat home. It's a sense of parting them, of course for short time.

"*Getting back home is mandatory*"; and the sweetest part of any expedition, small or big, is to head back home in an appropriate condition.

I can feel the uncertainty and a bit of fear in the apprehensive voice of Ranjana, my spouse, which is natural. As now we have been together since ten years, she has been used to my peripatetic waif nature.

Most beautiful part of this jaunt is that all the expedition members are well known and company of the veterans would really assure the successful accomplishment of this sojourn.

Lately, we got the news that sporadic corona cases have been reported in *Bhaba* valley, leading to complete lockdown there as it was allegedly declared as containment zone by the administration. Initially I was so obsessed with this trek that I thought about heading all alone, even if they turn me back from the very threshold of this valley, for the other team members were reluctant thus far. But gradually the other members agreed to proceed. Now we are six persons in total up to *Karra* pasture. And to explore more into deeper valleys, I am not all alone, experienced guide Mr Billu Wangpa will meet us at Karra.

All the quibbles and doubts about soloing had been quelled after I contacted Billu. I Hope it would be fun and enjoyment all together.

'Dr Ankush and Dr Pramod; my colleagues and hiking partners are on the way and procuring provisions. One team is waiting at Katgaon base camp, so nothing to fear or worry about. It's time to celebrate Independence Day (as we shall reach Karraon Independence Day eve) with complete freedom. Well! Would the mountains of mind be conquered along? I hope so'.

It would be my fifth sojourn through the sylvan beauty of this besotted valley. Unlike Ed Vistures or Veikka Gustaffsonthe veteran climbers, neither do I have any ambitions to conquer the big mountains, nor do I hike to seek magical wisdom. I also don't know much about flora and fauna of Himalayas as Billu does, but still I like to keep trotting in a trance like situation, while hauling a huge load all up the treacherous trails of perilous mountains. It's a kind of tacit call that I apprehend from mountain side, which I just can't ignore.

15.08.2020 11.30 PM *KARRA*

I picked up Rajeshwar from*Nigulsari* on 14.08.2020 around 11.00 am, while all the provisions and ration was procured by the two doctors at *Tapri*; though they missed a lot many things from my list including essential medicines. We reached *Katgaon* past noon. No sign of any lock downor restricted movement due to corona caseshere, as were much rumored around. Business was running as usual. Folk here seems more scared, not from the entry of any outsider but from random corona cases that erupted recently in one of the villages of this valley and was considered as a containment zone. Stigmatization is much worse than actual affliction in itself.

Staff members of our department were waiting for us here. A vehicle had already been hired till last motorable point.

After distributing ration evenly, we hauled our rucksacks to the trunk of *Bolero camper* and proceeded sharp at 2.00 PM. I tied the stove and small tent to my rucksack, which must be weighing around 25 to 30 kg.

A couple of ailing bovine cases were attended on the way, call of the duty! Well, livestock owner expect a lot from us and we never say no.

Road constructed by hydroelectric power company led us far away, just below *Gyaru* forest range, bypassing *Humti*pasture, our proposed camping site. As we were having sufficient time, we decided to reach up to *Mulling,* for camping would be blissful in that picturesque place. Sky was quite clear, sun still much away from horizon.

Somehow a communication was set up with Billu Wangpa, two days ago, who was discharging his duties at *Karra*. When I told him about my plans of loitering in the valley, he got excited. He told me that we can explore the *Lippu Khago* up above *Tia Basin,* past *Karra*pasture. Only a few has dared to venture out towards this treacherous terrain till date. That was really exhilarating, for it would not just be a trekking but an exploration in itself!

Had finally that day come, when we both shall explore together?

"Someday", he has assured me earlier. I was really happy that I somehow got in touch with him at the right time and was more enthralled being with him than guiding my own team, candidly. How selfish it sounds, but that's the truth!

The charm of being on *Bhaba Pin* pass yet again, was tepid in front of the exuberance of exploring an unknown pass, that also with experienced partner. Such selfishness was bound to happen.

As we moved past *Gyaru* forest range, we saw three figures distantly, creeping down gradually towards our direction. Someone yelled; that's Billu wangpa! I couldn't believe. How could this man betray me? Day before yesterday he told me that we will explore the hidden pass together and now he was abandoning! Something bad happened at his home? I kept guessing, till he reached close. He was completely tanned, lean bodied, much leaner than last we met with stubs of beards on his face for he was on these mountains for past many days or months? He was holding two long staves, one on each hand. After exchanging customary pleasantries he told that he has got some unavoidable work back at his home and he would be back soon day after tomorrow, giving much relief to me. He also told me that it would be we two only on the proposed expedition, for he himself knew nothing about the *Lippa* pass. I was thrilled again. It would be a memorable hike, I thought.

They told us that a few monks were camping at *Mulling* and they had made a huge bonfire for that night. We reached mulling around 6.00 PM and found that dozens of *lamas* were camping here, rising big fire as if performing a pious ceremony. We pitched our tents a bit away, for we were here not for spiritual purpose.

We were all finished with setting the camp by dusk but the exasperating thing was that the white kerosene that we carried from *Katgaon* was adulterated and we would soon be out of fuel at higher altitude. Fortunately, here firewood was in sufficient quantity as the tree line lies just beneath the valley and the previous hikers had thrown a few logs of dried wood around.

I took over the charge of cooking. We prepared special chicken, for it was Dr Ankush's marriage party, due for long. He has procured two bottles of *IMFL* (Indian Made Foreign Liquor) from *Kafnu* and it was time to open the corks. My headlamp was working efficiently. In fact it's a three-phase lamp, red light, low beam and high beam procured recently from *decathelon*. We enjoyed the blissful calm evening by sitting around big fire.

By 9 p.m. as we were teetering with intoxication we heard a lot of conundrum from nearby camp. A few school students have joined the monks for that night and it was gala time over there. Unable to resist ourselves, we soon reached the spot and joined the kids, dancing, whistling, and merry making in the wild. After sometime we sat down to play *antakshari.* These young kids proved beyond comparison. It was only the prowess of Dr Ankush who lyricized his own songs and gave it his melodious voice, deceiving the kids as if we were singing from some old Bollywood movies of 70's. The '*departmental song*' that he composed instantaneously was worth laughing.

It was late by 1 a.m. when we were finally done with *antakshari* and sluggishly swayed towards our camps. We chanted slogans of Independence. It was 73rd years of Independence. 'Are we really worth that'? I quibbled, as we retired for the day in that small cocoon of our ensconced tarpaulin.

Next morning I got up at 6 a.m. A bit of fog was swirling around but sky was clear. My head was banging considerably. That intoxication last night was the culprit. I couldn't enjoy the early morning view. I never felt like writing my almanac. Mr. Tara Chand (TC), our reliable pharmacist prepared hot tea. And we enjoyed *parathas* with sauce that had been packed previous day at *Katgaon.* But the headache persisted. Mr. Geeta Ram, Animal Husbandry Assistant and TC have planned to head down. For them journey was over.

At *Mulling* pasture, many animals are kept in open for grazing till late fall by the locals ritualistically. The nutritious high altitude grass not only increases their body weight but also make them fertile.

One jersey cow came near to our tent and guess, when I tried to milk her, she kept quite. I milked her enough to prepare tea at least for two times!

While breaking the camp the elastic chord of *three men tent* broke, putting a serious threat to our further camping up above. Moreover my *two men tent* got a nick on its top. We tried to fix the chord but of no use. Finally we decided to send it down instead carrying it up unnecessarily. Now Billu Wangpa's two men tent would be put to service.

We started our hike towards *Karra* at 9.00 am. Rajeshwar took the lead and soon he was out of sight. Dr Ankush started to trail.

At the final ascent to *Karra* he got completely exhausted. Rajeshwar babu came all the way down to carry his load. I retrieved a few heavy items from his rucksack and pushed it down insidemine. It must be weighing around 35 Kg now! But I felt comfortable. Dr Pramod was excelling well and seemed fit.

At around half past noon we were sitting comfortably at *Karra* camps. Again that sense of accomplishment erupted.

After taking a bath in nearby *bawdi* (natural water), that has been deftly crafted by local shepherds, we enjoyed *maggi* noodles and had a brief nap. Headache was all gone now. Crispy *pakoras* were being sauté in the mess. We enjoyed hot tea and *pakoras*. Ashok Kumar, Animal Husbandry Attendant from nearby*Kaksthal* camp (District Kinnaur), came with the news that one sheep from his flock has been attacked by a dog this morning and need some surgical intervention and they were eagerly waiting for us since morning. They had alsoprepared lunch for us in anticipation. A local medical surgeon was on trekking tour with his team and has pitched tent near to departmental camp. He had advised them to get the instruments for emergency surgery, as wind pipe of poor animal was damaged. We picked up a few medicines and instrument, and headed to the spot. After examination it was found a clear case of tracheal rupture, air swooshing through the lacerated wound at ventral cervical region. Shortly the surgeon also joined. We talked about the procedure and prognosis. We were not having any absorbable sutures. Luckily my first aid kit possessed curved cutting needles. With the help of simple thread we repaired the wound, last attempt to save one life. Surgeon Dr. Suneel was posted at Regional Hospital *Rekongpeo*. He is a young enthusiastic guy, obviously animal lover. He augured our efforts and we also put his expertise to use.

With the hope that this hapless animal would recover soon, it was time to enjoy the hospitality of *Kaksthal,* Kinnaur guys.

Dried game meat was ready and the local potion which I gulped to some limit though, proved sufficient to parry away the bitter late evening cold. Soon we were joined by medico and his team, all inebriated. It was gala time indeed. We sang songs, applauded each other and had lotsof fun. Finally we got back to our tent by 11.00 pm. It was time to retire. Earlier in the day I thought about pitching my own *two men tent* beside the permanent departmental tent, which other doctors were supposed to occupy, for I love my solitude; the basic purpose of being on the mountain. But then couldn't find appropriate place to pitch it. However I opened my own sleeping bag and slipped inside, to be embraced by deep slumber. For now it was proving convenient. No problem in sleeping.

16.08.2020 9.15 AM *KARRA*

'Got up at 6 a.m. in the morning. Answered nature's call. It is a bright clear sky. Had a look westward. Tia pasture and far above Lippa pass sprawls majestically; though clandestine beyond smaller peaks. I wish we cross it over or at least reach to its base next week. Physically finding the vigor undettered. Today will head to fustirang at around noon. Will halt there before final assault to Bhaba –Pin pass tomorrow early morning. Will carry only calculated provisions and ration. Hope all guys will make it to the top. Billu wangpa will reach by evening. Contemplating to explore Tia valley and that exhilaration continues. Time to enjoy the morning tea in a blissful serene environment'.

16.08.2020 8.37 PM *FUSTIRANG*

Cocooned in my ensconced liar, fully packed inside sleeping bag, after having sumptuous dinner of *Dal* and *Rice*,and of course a couple of pegs of local *Moori* that Rajeshwar has carried wisely, what else blissful can be than to enjoy the freedom in solace. Today's journey was a bit comfortable for we walked just 6 to 7 km from *Karra* to *fustirang*.

A broad picturesque valley *Fustirang*, may be considered as base camp for *Bhaba-Pin* Pass. Last time when I trekked solo from *Karra* to *Mudh,* I had my breakfast here down the stream and thereafter headed all the way up to pass, for I were worried about getting late. So in that rush couldn't enjoy the beauty of this pasture and also couldn't explore valleys deep within.

We started our hike sharp at noon today. We carried minimum of load that is needed essentially. I shed all the accessories including power bank and additional clothes. Ration was kept to minimum, up to two meals, one dinner and one breakfast. I also asked team members to shed all other unnecessary things which of course proved prudent. We reached here at 3 p.m. not much exhausted. I was glad that other two doctors made it comfortably. However an incident happened just at the base of this valley. Rajeshwar's sleeping bag, which was hanging with the hook outside his rucksack, got severed and before I could pounce over it to hold, it tumbled down all the way into the gushing downstream unabated and all we could do was to watch intently its flow down toward *kafnu* Dam. This may happen to any living being if one becomes a bit careless in such terrain.

After reaching this place I ransacked proper place to pitch the tent. Once we were done with securing the pegs, we prepared hot tea. A local shepherd also accompanied. There after duty of preparing *dal and rice* for dinner was assigned to both the doctors as myself and Rajeshwar ventured deep inside the valley to look after the shepherd to whom Billu wangpa has lent his portablr, round, light, *Kero*-stove, and he had asked to bring it back for *Lippa pass* expedition. We had bought two leather washers for his (shepherd's) non-functional kerosene stove pump so that he could repair it and give back the reliable Billu Wangpa's stove.

The valley inside is really beautiful. Thick numerous glaciers prevails up to the top and to the left side *Chhoti Jot* stands tall, which is also another pass to *Pin* valley. I wished someday I explore that as well.

After unsuccessful attempt to repair his stove I offered him mine and brought back Billu's. No headache, nausea or fatigue was appreciable at this moment. I had my reservations about other two doctors making it to the top. However, they prepared nice*dal*. We enjoyed the ritualistic potion before dinner.

'What a place and way to enjoy the dusk at this terrain with wafting fog and clear starry night sky. Temperature is just normal, not much coldness appreciable. Every moment I spent here is blissful. Tomorrow's plan is to get going by 5 a.m, though I knew it would not be before 6 a.m. Expected time to be on the top is 10:00 a.m. We will carry minimum of load for preparing Prasadam/ halwa at top. Breakfast will be bread, jam with tea to be relished on the way. Hope weather remains clear tomorrow. We will head back to Kara by tomorrow evening. It will be successful first stage, before the final serious exploration towards Lippa Pass starts. Rajeshwar is trying to sleep inside blanket hired from neighboring shepherd and gossips inside the other tent are audible no more. We are in the luxury of a comfortable tent and sleeping bags, at such heights and what we wish is to conquer the top tomorrow.

It's 9 p.m. All I can hear is the gushing sound of nearby glacial stream. It's time to retire for the day. My sleeping bag is working well for now. In fact I am using it for third consecutive night. I am remembering our staffers, Mr. Ashok and Mr. Ramesh, who helped us wholeheartedly to cross the cool stream just past Karra this afternoon. To cross a gushing stream that also past noon is really a heroic task. More so, bare feet, when water rises to knee heights and the flow is strong enough to stagger you down. Rather, it was more thrilling to cross the rivulet than to ascend the mountain itself. What a lovely guys, what a lovely team. Good night'

18.08.2020 8.16 AM *KARRA*

'Beautiful sunny morning after slight early morning drizzle. It's time to pack up after successful summit of Bhaba-Pin Pass yesterday. All our preparations and plan was executed well. It was an ultra light assault indeed. And the most exhilarating thing was that both our doctors especially Dr Ankush made to the top, without much serious problem. Weather remained crispy clear'.

As per our plan, I got up at 5 am. It was fog all around, so again crawled inside my sleeping bag. At 5.30 am slowly the fog settled and we could clearly see the steep shoulder, full of scree, to *Bhaba-Pin* Pass. Prepared tea and had light breakfast of bread and jam. We packed minimum of essentially needed thing with only two rucksacks each to be carried by Rajeshwar ji and me. All the ingredients required for preparing *prasadam* were packed, along with snacks and tea, which were to be relished mid-way. I also kept glucose powder inside my rucksack in case I need it.

Finally at 6.30 am we started the climb. The 'shoulder' consists of fine gravels brought down by glacier moraine. Early morning climb proved to be a wise decision. After one and a half hour we were almost on the ridge of this steep scree. Dr Ankush trailed but I kept him motivating consistently and he did followed up soon. Up on the mountain we encountered three big glaciers, which needed to be traversed. Candidly I hate walking over snow, reason yet not known. A beautiful sapphire glacial lake welcomed us just beneath the pass. I and Rajeshwar excelled ahead for my GPS battery was about to die and all I wanted to measure the exact distance between *Fustirang* and the Pass digitally. The mesmerizing lake and such beautiful aura couldn't be appreciated in my previous jaunt for, unlike this year, it did rain a lot that season melting away the glaciers. Ialong with Rajeshwar being in the front took a lot of photographs before climbing the pass and supplicating to Almighty for this successful ascent.

We collected the left over logs of wood and with the help of kerosene that we had carried along we lit the fire easily, which is quite a challenging task at such height. We prepared a delicious ghee sautéd *halwa* by the time both the doctors reached the top.

Valleys towards south were guarded by high dry mountains which I traversed two years ago in a single day. Towards the north it was glaciers all around.

Biggest reward of starting the day early was that we reached the summit at 9 am and before the fog started to shroud the vista and high cold wind blew, we were all done.

We spent almost three hours on the top. No sign of fatigue or headache was apprehended, rather a sense of accomplishment prevailed. However my entire focus was on next expedition towards *Lippu* Pass.

Descent from the top was a bit hard work, for the trail through moraine was really perilous. We had to clamber at the top of shoulder. We had a quick *maggi* lunch down at *Fustirang* before finally descending to *Karra*. Initially we thought about crossing a glacier mid-way, to catch a trail to the other end, which would lead us to *Karra* without crossing the rivulet, which by now would have become a torrent at this hour. But as the trail across glacier was perilous itself, we decided to take the normal route, for we could still rely over the services of Ashok and Ramesh.

It was an easy descent except the daunting task of crossing the gushing stream. Initially I tried to muscle my way across, but the flow was fierce to shiver the spine. Ashok came to rescue again and there we were lying comfortably inside the *Kaksthal* tent. Hot *masala* tea was served. Someone has spotted a silhouette walking with "four limbs" (two additional for staves) with acquainted pace toward our camp. And right they were in guessing. Billu wangpa was back.

It was time to celebrate the victory, of course on ourselves!

After evening gala at *Kaksthal* camp, we headed back to our *Jeori* (Shimla) departmental tents, at a walking distance. I slept cozily inside my sleeping bag. I am thankful to all the expedition members especially both the doctors who in turn accompanied out of the blue and also Mr. Rajeshwar negi who is too much dependable and a good climber indeed. It was really a great team work.

Scheduled departure time for tomorrow's *Lippa* Pass expedition is set to 9.30 am.

I got up at 6 am today. After sumptuous breakfast cum lunch (brunch, precisely, for in the departmental mess, full meal is served only twice in a day) it's time to part. Sky is pretty clear. Tia valley is majestically sprawling ahead. Doctors will head down to *Bhaba* valley as I will proceed toward deep *Tia* valley. It's going to be a learning expedition for me, as my reveries of accompanying the veteran Billu Wangpa are materializing today. I had packed my rucksack with needed gear and provision. Though I won't be able to match the pace of Billu Negi, but he seems pretty encouraging. He knowingly rejected the entry of a third member to this tour as he seems equally enthusiastic to explore as duo. Let's hope we make it to the *Lippa* pass and the beauties of these pristine valleys are explored and enjoyed up to hilt.

Twofer – II

STAGE 2, BHABA-LIPPA

18.08.2020 09.57 PM *TIA PLAIN*

'Tired to extreme. Just cocooned inside my sleeping bag, after having grand dinner, though smelly and maggot infested; sodden dry lamb at local shepherd's hut. We are moved by the shepherd's hospitality indeed. He felt very much sorry for such preparations, for he couldn't cure it properly. But the weather was all to be blamed. I saw a few maggots scrawling through the rosary of dried meat hanging just above the fire place. I could have vomited my intestines out, but the hunger and hospitality kept me reticent and calm'.

Today we started our journey from *Karra* at 10.45 am, almost an hour late than scheduled time. I reached the starting point of our journey, campsite of *Kaksthal* farmright on time i.e. 9.30 am, bidding farewell to my team members, which headed down to Kafnu (Kinnaur) after successful *Bhaba Pass* trek. But the departmental staff over here must have partied hard till late night hence obviously got up late. They were having breakfast and thereafter packed up their rucksacks. Three more local guys accompanied us up to *Tia*.

Till last evening it was all a *duo* expedition, but by morning one more fellow, Mr. Gauri Shankar Kaushal *aka* Badshah bhai also got included. Billu Wangpa asked me if we could include him. For we were carrying only a *two men* tent hence he would has to carry extra one with additional ration. He was excited to join us to the extent that he told he will carry all paraphernalia including fuel and *Kero* stove himself. To me it's always three better than two. 'Badshaah' as he is called by *Kaksthal*staff, is a short guy of about 4 feet 10 inches height with disheveled hair and grotesque dressing sense. He is strongly built and wore fancy slippers all the while and hung his gum boots on the back of his rucksack. But indeed he is a tough, exploration loving freak, which I noticed later.

At *Tia* we reached about half past one. It's a quite wide river basin with lots of pasture land around. Its beauty is more revealing than *Karra* itself. Towards the north lies snowy peak *Hans Bastion* which is still allegedly unclimbed. As per Billu Wangpa, latest expedition by ITBP didn't succeed to conquer it. One gushing stream, *Kirkas (Lippu Khad*) has to be crossed here in order to traverse towards the pass. By this hour it has become a torrent. So instead of crossing it we decided to explore its right bank towards *Lippu* Pass with the hope that we may encounter some glacier up above, thus bypassing the roaring stream.

We met a shepherd on the way who told us that he hadn't ventured too far into the valley and do not know about glacier if any. However his partner, who was away tending livestock, sometimes takes his flock deep inside valley thus may help us. We hiked through treacherous terrain having slope 70 to 80 degrees, putting each foot cautiously one behind another. For if we make any mistake we will roll down to deep gorge not visible beneath, without a halt. Even to take rest I had to lean my weight completely over the slope, without having a glimpse downward, for I was turning giddy and to some extent was repenting my move.

Shortly we met the shepherd, who signaled us from the top that there is no vantage in moving ahead. Billu Wangpa muscled his way up to shepherd; while I was thinking that why the hell he is not coming down to us? We were high above the gorge in a very precarious terrain. A few horses were grazing gaily below. No shrubs or thick grass was visible around to catch hold. The shepherd was known to Billu. He regretted not coming down. He said there is a glacier over gorge, visible from next ridge but the final stretch up to it is too much dangerous. While listening to it, I thought how much can be '*too much dangerous*', and what we are standing at right now? Isn't it too much dangerous? Even his goats do not venture to this stretch. We were having sufficient time till daylight fade but given the vigorous flow especially in the afternoon, crossing the *Tia* stream was out of question for the day.

Finally we decided to give it a try. I was really dithering while having a gaze downward. The steepness was just increasing. I was scared even of getting back to *Tia* base. Billu and Badshah kept on moving ahead in search of any possible trail up to glacier. Shortly we could see the big glacier up the valley and beautiful barren base of high mountain range and possible pass above it.

This trek is not explored so far, hence no one including the shepherdwas much sure about terrain up above. Recently three young local guys of *Bhaba* valley has dared to cross over to *Asrang* village via this pass, and they crossed it successfully. So hope was there for us. We had planned just to reach to the top of this Pass and get back as local folk of that valley were not allowing anybody to enter their village due to corona scare.

After finding the glacier and beautiful landscape up above, Billu wangpa and Badshah got pumped up. The route up to glacier was however too much treacherous as we have to negotiate rocky, loosely adhered water smeared terrain with uncertain consistency standing at 75 degree inclination. In addition to this, a rough scree zone of 200 meters also had to be negotiated.

As I gazed the possible path, I shuddered top to toe. Adrenaline was literally oozing from every pore of my body. While the other two were planning to give it a try I was shrugged and bewildered. For it seems too much perilous task. It would be one on one. You cross you survive, you make a mistake, and all is over. I never thought about getting into such situation so early. Barely do we knew each other, it's not even 24 hours of our interaction and here I was to follow their risk taking limits, which may vary individual to individual. But then turning back at this point was also not pragmatic. As they discussed the probabilities, I kept mum, as if mumbling tacitly *No, No, No. It's a wrong decision, let's turn back*!

Two person's decision was outweighing mine. Billu Wangpa must have apprehended my condition and asked if I can follow them; all empty, for they would climb the section along with my load and further would repair the trail through scree zone. Somehow I got ready after their reassurance, watching the route constantly. A small mistake would be the last moment, I knew. While getting down to the point where we had to negotiate the rocky terrain I lingered with thoughts that why we had taken such a stupid step? Why the hell we didn't trylong conventional route? What was the need to hurry? For God sake we had got sufficient provision and there was no dearth of time.

At one point I sat down while other two moved ahead. I remembered everyone. God, my family, my friends and what not? Bliss would be to reach at the ridge just above glacier, but then the cost was your life. No ropes no anchors, no ice axe and no appropriate staves. I considered it as a suicide.

As Badshah was asked to *rekkie* the final rocky terrain, we waited till he hounded the route and came back with the news that it wasnegotiable. It was 3.30 pm and throughout day we had already climbed a great distance, so the muscles were fatigued and gushing river below was gaping at us ghastly. All of a sudden, Billu Wangpa signaled to head back, for he knew taking risk with me would be an unwise step considering my less expertise. And also Badshah's assessment was not reliable. I was relieved to the extent that I construed it as rebirth. Candidly the steepness of this terrain looked a piece of cake while heading down to *Tia* basin.

At last we reached the basin at 5.00 pm and set up the camp. I was tired to the extreme. We prepared tea and enjoyed *Maggi* thereafter. I was assigned Billu Wangpa's tent all alone, and the two will lie down together in mine. For dinner we would move up to nearby shepherd's *dera* as Billu had told him that we would be their guests if we won't be able to reach the glacier. Their tent was visible and they must have acknowledged our return. They had already advised us to take the conventional route. With the scheduled time of departure at 6.00 am I was just trying to get some rest.

Tia is a beautiful place indeed. On the way we found various high altitude floras. Billu Wangpa has very much knowledge about it. He told me their scientific name with traditional uses. Badshah also showed me, *Jadi dhoop, Jungli ajwaain, Kadwi, Jungli kakdi. Kadwi*is a medicinal plant which local folk is looking after for its market value here at *Katgaon* is Rs 1500 per Kg dried, as told by Badshah. Locals with their family members are camping up in this terrain to dig it out for days. I also collected a couple of small roots and packed it in my rucksack. Many more things to be learnt in coming days but I swear I would relinquish the expedition if come across such situation again. *Getting to the top is optional but getting back home is mandatory.* Sleeping all alone in the tent, only gushing rivulet audible and those irritating donkey brays intermittently.

19.08.202 05:10 AM *TIA BASIN*

It was a good night sleep. I slept on a single mattress all alone inside two men tent of Billu wangpa. Today got up at 5.00 am, sky a bit cloudy. No feel of coldness throughout night was observed. Outside tent, it's fog all around. We had to cross the rivulet as early as possible. Badshah had not reached yet, for he rested at local shepherd's *dera* last night, as he had mistaken Billu Wangpa's folded mattress as spare sleeping bag so he had to arrange a blanket from shepherd, to negotiate coldnight uphill. He would also bring the *ghee* smeared *chappatis* prepared by benevolent shepherds, to be relished with tea on the way. I had to prepare tea.

'My hands still smell awful, thanks to last night's sordid meat. I am feeling a bit fresh today. Hope all goes well and weather remains clear. Yes, of course missing my family especiallymy son. Rest everything is fine. Time to pack up'.

19.08.2020 09:16 PM High Camp 4800 meters, somewhere below *LIPPU PASS*

A drizzle has started right now. Quite cold outside, however prepared dinner, Dal & Rice, beside a small glacier. It took almost 4 hours to cook Dal (Mix of Malka & Dhulle Maah). Wind was not that much high in the evening and star lit night in this barren terrain just added to the beauty.

We started from *Tia* basin at 7.15 am, trailing scheduled time. River was crossed after due diligence, for the water was freezing cold and reached up to waist at few points. I always found it difficult to keep my bare feet stable on small sharp gravels under forcefully rushing water. Only Billu Negi showed the courage to take the lead and goaded us to other side. He told us later that he is not scared to such crossing, for he had survived twice after sweeping in such streams during his childhood! His twin staves with metal tips proved lucrative in such situation; whereas my wooden stick was quite blunt at the end, so gave away under such forcible water currents. I wonder how high the rise in water level would have been after noon!

Route from conventional side is quite good. It's a gradual ascent toward *Dulmangch,* the last *Dera* of shepherds. A beautiful camping site it is, overlooking the glacier and way to pass above. We reached the only glacier across river soon and crossed it by 11am.

Now shortly, we were at the site where two valleys meet up above. We rested briefly and had breakfast of bread, Jam with hot tea. Hereafter the aura changed completely. It's all boulders and morains brought down by huge glaciers over a period of time. I kept the pace slow and steady, and didn't encountered fatigue mid way. Billu Wangpa however took another route to explore the adjoining valley. We had to cross four rivulets today. I and Badshah kept moving constantly along the glacial bed beside the stream. In the morning, while crossing river, at one point of time Badshah was almost swept away in gushing river, when Billu Wangpa finally came to his rescue. I found much difficulty in traversing the scree, for every two steps ahead, I kept slipping one back.

At 2pm we pitched high camp at this place. Now just above this camp, two valleys opens up, one to right and another to left. From down hills, a ridge at eastern valley is seen partly, so we thought it to be the Pass. On reaching this point, Billu wangpa told that we should try to *rekkie* the western valley. May be his sixth sense say so.

At, 3.45 pm, after having *maggi* lunch with *ghee* smeared *chappatis* (thanks to magnanimous shepherds) and some rest; we went for reconnaissance of the valley leftward with minimum luggage. I felt difficulty again negotiating scree and glaciers up above. Most of the glaciers here are blackish blue, implying they stood here for tens of centuries. I was tired and trailing behind both the guys. Billu was leading with same enthusiasm and encouraging us. He was showing his strength at such altitudes as he galloped past us with small back pack.

The fog has started to shroud the area. We couldn't see the terrain around and in such conditions reconnaissance was just useless in my opinion. We couldn't saw Billu Negi and his footprints on glacier so we kept waiting on big boulder at a vantage point. I thought about turning around. Badshah was of same opinion. It was a whiteout, visibility just few meters. We had decided 5.30 pm as time to turn around in any case, down to the base camp. Now we got scared, for Billu wasn't giving any response to our calls and whistles. There were glaciers all around, which seem non-negotiable. Hard blue ice!

We couldn't dare to traverse this blue ice searching him, for there may be crevasses ahead. Had something bad happened to him? We rebuked him, for his behavior was abominable. He should have waited for us at least, till we came to view. I ventured a bit leftward over big boulder to look for any sign. Nothing worth climbing! Where in the hell had he gone? We waited, till set time to return. Then came the voice and whistle from direction we couldn't appreciate. We took a sigh of relief, for it wasn't a SOS. Actually he has just moved ahead on the glacier at which we were resting, through a small gully which led him all the way to the Pass ahead. So he was yelling eureka, and directing us to follow him. We couldn't find his footmarks and the gully was shrouded again by fog. So at 5.30 pm sharp, we turned back.

Shortly Billu negi conjured from fog with utmost happiness on his face, for he has just found the Pass. We all were exhilarating for we need not to astray tomorrow in search of *Lippa* Pass.

How close we were today!

Billu's face was blushing with happiness which he deserves immensely.

We descended gradually to the base camp, feeling jubilant. So tomorrow we will head again toward the Pass and then will explore the other valley, before finally heading down to *Tia* basin.

19.08.2020 10.36 PM HIGH CAMP *LIPPU PASS*

'Too much tired but I am happy that I didn't encounter any headache above 5000msl. It's drizzling outside and out tent is just at the base of a scree laden protuberance. Not a safe place to pitch a tent actually, more so in such weather, for any rock may roll down, anytime. Hope this rain shall stop shortly and a clear sky we encounter tomorrow. At times I missed

my family a lot. I remembered my mother. I was happy for if something bad happen to me, I will be close to her, otherwise with my loving family. I thought about it many a times on the way. We are just on a secluded barren place, no one else has ventured here for decades and perhaps no one camped here ever. Time to get some rest'.

20.08.2020 06.13 AM HIGH CAMP *LIPPU PASS*

What an incredible view it was from my high altitude camp just below the moraine leading to *Lippu* Pass. It did rain throughout night. It was overcast sky with fog smitten aura. Night was quite cold. Couldn't sleep soundly for I was worried about any rock fall due to this rain. In early morning heard a big thundering sound east ward, where some chunk of glacier must have broken. All alone in my tent, cold was expected to be experienced. Now the home sickness has started. More the day passes away from home with more of the perils in mountains, more I feel nostalgic. It's almost about two weeks from home and seventh consecutive day sleeping inside tent.

'For me reaching the top is not mandatory but to reach back home safely is. Have to cross big boulders, scree zone, gushing streams, precariously dangling glaciers and dangerous trails. We are supposed to rekkie another valley above, only after reaching the pass today. Billu Wangpa repaired an old cairn there yesterday. It's still drizzling intermittently. How are we supposed to move up in this condition? Inside other tent these two guys are contemplating to head back. Even to descend amid rain is not much safer and to stay here

inside tent, just below cracked glacier, is not wise. Preparing breakfast over Kerosene stove is cumbersome. So all we can do is just wait and watch. It seems mountain want to check our patience, for it is not prepared to let us in, yet. My nails had grown longer and dirty, beards grayish and hair disheveled. Skin completely tanned. Didn't take bath for past 5-6 days, may be stinking, but that's the life in mountains. Thankfully the weather remained clear so far and we did climbed Bhaba-Pin pass and up to this point blissfully. If weather permits us to reach the pass today we will head back gaily down to Tia basin. Let's hope we complete everything satisfactorily. To me, even if we get down right now, it's fine, for we had almost reached the pass yester evening. What if we could not see the cairn and valleys toward Lippa side! I will consider this expedition as a success, even not expected by myself, to reach so far. Hope we make either way soon. Time to get relieved'.

20.10.2020 07.11 PM *TIA BASIN*

'Wow! A real sense of satisfaction prevails amid the constant din of gushing Kirkass and Kasholing Khad (streams). I am finally sitting inside my ensconced liar of two men Coleman tent though occupying it alone. No sign of any coldness or throbbing heartbeat anymore, for we had finally conquered the Lippa Pass. Yes we did it. It was drizzling all the day; fine droplets visible with wafting fog'.

I got up at 7:30 a.m. finally, for I couldn't resist having a final look at the condition outside. For once we thought of getting all the way down. It was intermittent white out. By 8 o'clock our breakfast was ready. Last evening's *dal-rice* was warmed and *Maggi* was prepared. Hot tea served thereafter. By 9 O'clock we made the final assault. It was not prudent to get back after coming so close to the Pass. A try was indeed expected. As per Billu Wangpa, it would be just 15 minutes climb from the point we reached last evening. I and Badshah proceeded first with all fresh legs. I didn't slip over scree or glacier even for once today. No sign of headache was observed. Without any halt intermittently and with constant speed we reached upto the final glacier in just 42 minutes. With each step I felt confident and blissful. Mild drizzle was also there which later turned to minuscule snowflakes. Billu Wangpa started late and wasn't seen behind. We headed in the direction that was told by him. We found the footprints and metal tip marks on ice. We followed it over the giant glacier and there in the fog we could see the chorten.

Bravo! We made it. I made a small video with my cell phone. We yelled in extreme ecstasy, supplicated beneath the cairn and remembered and thanked Almighty.

Toward the other side we could see a cauldron of huge glacier and two beautiful blue lakes sprawling majestically. Soon Billu Wangpa joined and we three raised our hand making sign of victory. All the fatigue and tiredness was gone. It felt all fresh. We thought about getting down toward other side but then the way was too much treacherous. Badshah told about making a cairn beside the old one and soon we were collecting icy wind-crafted stones as Billu started the masonry work. The wind towards Bhaba valley was cold and intense, however towards Lippa side, gone at all. Sharp contrast of atmosphere was appreciable similar to *Bhaba-Pin* Pass. After *Pooja* and *Pratishtha* of new chorten, we kept waiting for fog to settle so that we may appreciate the Lippa valley downwards. The swirling mist quelled only momentarily and the view was ethereal.

After an hour around 11:15 a.m. we decided to head back. Now I wasn't scared of walking over glacier or scree. All the horror was gone. I even felt like skiing down the glacier like Billu, but stopped for the lack of appropriate long staves. I saw many small cairns erected along the margins of huge glacier, depicting path downward. I made them yester evening and felt really happy. I remembered mum again and wished she is happy and fine wherever she lives now. I wished she hovers freely and gaily wherever she wants.

On our way down towards the base of glacier Billu Wangpa was waiting for us as he skied his way down past us, asking to explore the valley toward right side. But Badshah was a bit reluctant to move further and rather wanted to get back to high camp as soon as possible, for he was drenched completely and this is how you feel when ill prepared. I wore raincoat and gloves (thanks to Dr Ankush) and my clothes over torso were dry at least. I liked the plan of Billu to explore a bit, for we were having sufficient time.

The valley opened up after moving over big boulders brought down by glaciers on the way. Soon I got tired and the Pass or for that matter any ridge wasn't seen due to constant fog and drizzle.

As Billu Wangpa headed further, I and Badshah turned around. There was no fun in exploring another Pass in such conditions. We reached high camp and prepared hot tea. We covered the make shift kitchen with raincoat and I prepared fried rice. Soon the drizzle turned into full-blown rain. I told Badshah to take rest inside tent for he was completely drenched and dripping through cloths. We relished lunch inside my tent as Billu joined us late at 2:30 p.m. He had found another pass opening just to the other side of twin lakes that we saw earlier. We all were happy. Mission was accomplished.

By 3:30 p.m. we had broken the camp and packed all the trash to be brought back to *Karra* for appropriate disposal. Our high camp stood at 4800 metres. As per Billu Negi, it was one of the highest elevations for camping, in his career. The Pass stood at 5200 meters approx.

Downward journey was blissful. We crossed only two streams on the way. Rain was consistent. Billu talked about different flora and fauna of this region, with its scientific name. I was very much moved by his knowledge about wildlife.

Against our estimated time of three hours to reach down to *Tia* basin it only took two hours. Here we were welcomed by local shepherd as they served hot tea immediately. Further journey couldn't be imagined at this hour as *Lippu Khad* was at its extreme. We pitched our tents beside its bank and enjoyed the hospitality of local shepherds.

'After devouring tasty dried goat meat (cured properly this time) I am just getting back to my tent. We played cards to pass the time. It's still raining outside. Gushing Khad's sound is deafening. No sign of coldness or fatigue. We are happy and

planning to have a complete circumnavigation of this Bhaba-Lippa Pass soon'.

To me it was really an awesome expedition. I came from home with a thought that I would venture in the mountains for a week without anyone accompanying, but I never thought that I would get so strong team.

It was at Twofer to me. The thrill was at extreme even at the beginning of this expedition when we tried to negotiate the perilous rocky trail above *Tia* basin. I swore I will never make such trip again, but gradually all my dread was gone. I am thankful to both the doctors, Billu Wangpa, Badshah, Departmental staff at *Karra* and to all those local shepherds who take life so much casually. It's my seventh night in sleeping bag, which had become my true friend indeed. I find myself most comfortable inside its cozy coverings.

This tour taught me many lessons. I know my family back home will be very much concerned about my whereabouts, for my last communication with them was more than a week ago. Yes I know; I am very much selfish but then more I go away from them, more I miss them, and more I love them.

'Tomorrow early morning we will cross the river and reach Kara, then it's time to celebrate the successful jaunt, for only a very few people know about the way to Lippa Pass and we have got our names embellished in this list and rather we know two passes up above. All the social obligations will be back by tomorrow, I don't know what's happening in professional life and family life. Hope I will manage all the things next week or two. I ought to call lovely better half tomorrow in any case for

she has been bestowed upon so much of responsibilities, before the whole world knows that I was again on the mountain. Does it matter to anyone? I never knew.

Time to retire for the day'.

21.10.2020 05.49 AM *TIA BASIN*

It was rain, rain and rain outside. I slept soundly last night, only to be woken up by some blunt force on the side of my tent. Must be some nearby inquisitive sheep/ goat or may be a dog! It feels as if monsoon is here, again. This untimely rain is going to be detrimental in some form. The flow of rivulet is high. We have to cross not just this *Khad*, which has swollen to a river but also streams just in front of *Kara* camps. The earlier, the better. This rain will continue for next few days so in my opinion better to keep on descending all the way down to *Kafnu* and back home. It would have been enjoyable to stay back at *Kara* for one day celebrating the successful expedition, but then with such conditions around, I find no fun & wisdom to do so. Let's see what happen next. Right now all we are focused about is crossing the stream. Night long rain only contributed to its magnitude. Hope this last step towards the final success of expedition will be safe and equally enjoyable.

22.10.2020 10:49 AM *HOMTE BRIDGE*

'We are waiting for 'Sharma ji' on Homte Bridge, after descending all the way from Kara. We have been stranded here for more than an hour as my car was left in the custody of Sharma ji, who is untraceable as of now!'

We started back journey today early morning at 6:45 a.m. exactly 45 minutes late than its scheduled time. Got up at 5:30 a.m. when Billu Wangpa shed away the sleeping bag. Slight mist was there but after sometime weather cleared up. Sunshine was in plenty and *Kara* valley was mesmerizing again. To move away from this valley is really heartbreaking. I bid adieu to Billu Wangpa, Ashok, Badshah and all the staff members. We had a light breakfast of *egg bhurji* at *Jeori* camp and started back with Khanna Babu, another pharmacist.

Yester morning journey from *Tia* to *Kara* was full of thrill. To cross the river was one of the greatest challenges, more so at early morning. We crossed it with goose bumps at 7 a.m. Even local shepherds were trembling with fear. At one point of time I felt like I will be swept away. Cold glacial water was more than enough to numb the body. Amid mild drizzle and fog we reached Kara at 10:00 a.m. A strange sense of accomplishment prevailed, as we celebrated with high five. All the members at base camp were thrilled. Earlier, I thought about descending all the way down to *Kafnu*, but then weather and the affection of staffers changed my mind. A siesta was highly deserved. We had brunch and went for some nap. In the evening, went towards the point of mobile signal and the gate that I had closed seven days ago been finally opened. News of our successful expedition filled Ranjana with extreme ecstasy and hope.

In the evening we had sumptuous dinner at *Jeori* farm camp and went for night rest at *Kaksthal* camp, where, after playing card briefly it was time to retire.

To part with these lovely guys especially Billu wangpa, was like missing something much closer to me. My heart plunged into deep melancholy, for we have lived through every thick and thin of this expedition, through life and death moments. May be this sense prevails due to our common thoughts and likings. Yes his knowledge and skills regarding climbing the high altitude is unmatchable and also his vigor and enthusiasm inexplicable, but at the core of his heart he is just a humble, self-contemplating creature. He does take risks as told by many of his colleagues, at times, which he acknowledge with utmost humility, but then life in such terrain is always risky.

Only moderate risks will lead to the beauty of these natural wonders, and by the way 'Risk' in itself is a comparative term. Isn't it?

This trip was not just a trekking but an exploration, for only a few had dared to reach up the pass that also not much recently. But we mapped the area and left some marks up above in form of huge cairns. Over all, it was just an awesome trip of this season and memorable one with the veteran.

It's Time to move back to civility. Still waiting for 'Sharma ji' ....

Women: As Hiking Companion

Off late I had turned to be a feminist, or perhaps that gender sensitivity was nurturing from childhood, for I was brought up in an environment where I was fostered in the absence of any female child. As I grew up, the inquisitiveness of probing the thoughts and life of fairer sex only increased, but due to lack of any proximity with opposite gender even at school or college level, those reveries couldn't be materialized.

Gender bias is much more prevalent in our society especially amongst the rural and less educated one. Even, some so called elite people, wielding scepter in the echelon of power and prestige, also discriminate not just outsiders but even their family members. Even now, most of the tough looking tasks are meant to be all male affairs, be it fighting for the nation, riding a bike or climbing a mountain etc.

When I took over the hobby of scaling mountain, little did I thought that I would be trekking some day with all women members, for it's all fun of boys to venture out, taking risks and show masculinity. This notion was further boosted when I met my inamorata who had all other common likings except walking on foot even for few hours leave aside for days together. As I increased my intensity of exploring the Himalayas, most of the time it was with male guides and friends. On summiting a pass, smoking pipe with male buddies was highly blissful and a sign of sheer strength and man hood. To take female members along was considered like taking a liability uncalled for. Many thoughts prevailed like we won't be able to concentrate over our goals, we may have to haul the load all by our selves, midway, when the lady wanderlust would relinquish everything and ought to be goaded all the way to top, etc. etc.

Recently, I heard about an all women expedition as early as 1970 when they climbed a peak somewhere in *Lahaul* (HP) and named it *Lalana*, which means 'women' in Bengali. Those days, mountaineering was an all-male affair, at least in India. On August 26, 1970, five days after they summitted *Lalana,* Ms. Guha and Ms. Saha were dead, swept away by the frigid fast flowing waters of a high altitude stream fed by five glaciers. Only one lady survived to tell the tale but this was really a motivational and daring task performed by Indian women of that era.

Recently one peak in Manali, *Hampta pass* region has been named after sexagenarian Nalini Sengupta, the veteran lady mountaineer, who has scaled several summits till now and had the honor of Himalayan peak 5260 christened after her as 'Mount Nalini', to salute her efforts to inculcate the thrill of mountaineering in youngsters since 1970.

Equally sensual was the reference and tale of Nanda Devi Unsoeld, the daughter of William Unsoeld, an

American mountaineer who was a member of the first American expedition to summit Mount Everest in 1963. He was possessed with Nanda Devi Mountain to the extent that he named his daughter after it. As father inherited his genes to his daughter, she also turned to be a mountain lover. Soon the father-daughter duo would venture out in Himalayas together.

On one such Indo-American expedition to Mt Nanda Devi in the year 1976, led by her father, at camp 4, she fell ill. Willie wrote,

"7 September was a pure blizzard at Camp 4 and none of us moved from the camp… However that night was bad one for Devi. Her stomach generated gas in such quantity that she simply couldn't sleep and spent most of the night sitting up to belch it forth. By morning she was extremely tired …… We were packed for departure, when at 11:45 a.m. Devi was suddenly stricken. She has time only to say with great calm, I am going to die, before she lapsed into unconsciousness. We tried mouth-to-mouth resuscitation but with no sign of success. Within 15 minutes I felt her lips growing cold against mine and I knew that we had lost her."

The tragedy took place at 7315m/ 24000 feet, making it impossible to bring back the body. So they (Willie Unsoeld and Andy Harvard, her fiancé) bundled her in a sleeping bag and slipped over the precipice of north east face. Later Dr Unsoeld said that they had 'committed her to the deep'.The *Giving Goddess* has taken her own.

During 1981 the Indian Army expedition made a successful ascent of both the main and East peaks simultaneously and placed a memorial stone for Nanda

Devi Unsoeld at the high altitude meadow *Sarson Patal.* An extract from her last diary was inscribed on the stone,

"I stand upon a windswept ridge at night with the stars bright above and I am no longer alone but I waver and merge with all the shadows that surround me. I am a part of the whole and am content." She was just 22. This is revered by all climbers for it's not just a tragic story but inspirational one.

Chantal Mauduit was a noted female French alpinist. She was known not just for her beauty but for her love and passion for mountains. Those days very few women climbers were into this so-called serious affair of topping the world. Her reference came in my recently read book, *No shortcut to the top* written by legendary American Alpinist Ed Viestures. In his words, (on 1992 K2 expedition)

"... *Besides being a good mountaineer Chantal was a gorgeous woman. She had long wavy brown hair. She always seemed vibrant and happy, even carefree. Everybody liked her, she was very flirtatious. She had this way of laughing as she looked at you and you would wonder if she was giving me that eye or is she this way with everybody. You can bet that every guy had his eyes on her."*

Little did I found any reference about her determination to summit the peak, or the sheer insatiable hunger of exploring the perilous mountain irrespective of her gender.

I read many books of legendary mountaineers across nation and all were having burning zeal of conquering one mountain after another. Never did I found any text or quote about similar burning zeal of a female counterpart, at least from the pen of fellow male climber.

At one point of time in his book Ed wrote about Chantal, after he and Scott Fischer aborted their own plan to successfully summit K2 in order to rescue her,

"*...I went to bed, lying in my bag with my Walkman headphones on, listening to Little Feat... all of sudden I felt somebody pulling on my foot. 'What's up? Oh, I just wanted to come and say goodbye.' Chantal answered. 'I am leaving tomorrow'.Meanwhile she was crawling farther and farther inside my tent, so I kind of knew what was going on, but at the same time I thought when does something like this ever happened? ... I was still dazzled by it all the next day, as I wrote in my diary, '...How could I refuse such a beautiful woman and it was a fun night and she reluctantly left at 5 a.m. What a gorgeous women!'...All through breakfast I kept surreptitiously plucking Chantal's long brown hairs off my fleece jacket which we had used as pillow. Nobody noticed. Only Scott knew about it, He looked at me and said, "So Ed, big tits or small tits?" I just cracked up. With all that clothing on, you can't really tell." ...I wondered that if I would ever see her again.*"

She died during one of her expedition on Dhaulagiri mountain along with her *Sherpa* guide inside her tent, for her burning desires of conquering the beast would not have been fulfilled. But in my mind her memory was more regarding that night, except others.

Vijay Lakshmi, one of my staffer a local woman, is also a mountain lover, even when her physique is reciprocal to her fantasies. She always keeps on appreciating my hiking activities through social media and in person as well. On my *Hamta* Pass Trek last year, she wished that she and her friends could join us some day.

This year due to Corona COVID confinement, those reveries of scaling a peak only bolstered. Even being a local girl she never explored *Kanda* of her own valley. So it was a perfect time to give some wings to her dreams. To me it's always a win-win situation if someone joins, irrespective of gender. But things kept on postponing as does happen with men folk. Men can get ready for any expedition even at the eleventh hour but for female it's not that much easier, more so for married women with kids at home.

For the fall was about to set, all plans for a hike was looking grim and I was much busy with my blogging work lately, so when she called me and told me about her proposed journey starting the very next day, I couldn't believe. I thought it would also get postponed like previous occasions. But this time her words sound resolute. I inquired about other team members and she told me it was all women team, her sister and sister's friend. Earlier I told her that I have no issues with girls if they can take their own responsibility and have *Will* to show endurance till extreme. But now as itinerary was set I got a bit perplexed. How would I cope with these women completely stranger to me? What shall I do in case someone falls in serious trouble? How shall I talk to them on the way? Where shall we sleep? How shall I relieve myself in privacy, and other kind of nonsense but pragmatic worries. The only thing that reassured me was my solo expedition previously, for I survived alone and here I was with other human beings at least. So without any hesitation I nodded to proceed as per plan and who knows some other Chantal Mauduit may arise! Whims of Men folk!

At 3 p.m. on 09-09-2020 we were at the point of proposed rendezvous, just above village *Kashpo*, *Nichar* valley, Kinnaur and full one hour behind schedule time. The two other women team members were waiting with their small rucksacks.

Ms. Sarasvati aka Saru, Vijayalakshmi's younger sister is Horticulture Development Officer at *Nichar*. Her physique and thick round glasses only bolstered my reservations about taking them to top. Her demure demeanor exalts further for even when she speaks it's hard to hear.

Her friend Ms. Bindu is also a Horticulture and Forestry graduate presently working with plantation drive of Public Works Department, government of HP. She looks a bit more robust and her oriental eyes seem more determined and focused towards the goal.

We exchanged the mandatory pleasantries and it was time to proceed. I hardly knew about them, there likings, their thoughts about me, or for that matter about hiking. Does that really matter? I wonder. They were talking in local dialect which was well beyond my comprehension. Vijay took the lead, for she had already been to *Chhot Kanda* previously. Both the girls followed her and I took the sweeper position, all the while thinking about journey, risks involved and of course Chantal Mauduit. From the very first ascent through *Kashpo* jungle it became evident that these ladies were tough not only physically but mentally as well. We rested briefly only about a couple of times and within one and half an hour we had crossed the bottleneck. Even Surat *maam,* our staffer at *Nichar*, whose son was about to accompany us later, had told me that with women trekkers along it may take three to four hours up to *Chhot kanda*. By that standard our speed was appreciable.

I talked barely en route and was more engrossed in my own thoughts. We reached *Chhot Kanda* at 6 p.m. We had taken provisions and ration along, for we would cook our own food on firewood as my Kerosene stove had not yet arrived from *Bhaba* valley.

Sunil, the son of our staffer caught us just near to *Chhot Kanda*. A young promising, strongly built, tall guy, a previous Merchant Navy fellow, he seems jovial and courteous as well. He told us that he also love hiking and in fact was looking for some hiking freaks to explore the valleys around.

Chhot Kanda is a picturesque place situated amid thick conifer forest capped with green high alpine pastures. For tonight Sunil would be our host. As we took rest inside small but beautiful home of Sunil at *Chhot Kanda*, his mother told us that it would be appropriate to leave as early as midnight to appreciate beautiful morning view of the *Pabang* (valley). I was a bit perplexed to know that, for I had never done any night hiking ever before. The hospitality of Sunil and his family was just awesome.

Young kids Chintu and Akki were so happy that they kept rocking around. We slept at 10:30 p.m. and Sunil told me that we have sufficient time to rest for 2 hours and 5 minutes precisely!

Sleep wasn't expected but I woke up only to the alarm bell set by Sunil on his smart phone. Breakfast was already packed after dinner, thanks to the ladies of our group. We had already packed our bags before taking rest. As we moved out of our room, I notices a bright star lit sky with ample moonlight. At 1:15 a.m. we started the hike. I was half sleeping, half awake. As Sunil was leading the group, I heard some growl toward small brook flowing beside the trail. Moon was crescent but still the darkness prevailed through the thickets of forest. Sunil immediately yelled as it was the sound of Himalayan black bear replete in this region. No wonders, considering the thickness of forest, wild animal were expected around. He unzipped his rucksack and took out Bluetooth speaker.

In the dead of night, five trekkers were hiking quietly, listening to the local Kinnauri songs. At times we whistled and shouted so that wild animal if any would be scared away.

After arduous hike of around 5 kilometers tree-line finished and we were standing on white moon lit *bugyal.* A sheep flock was stationed a little distance away. It was 3:15 am. Wind was cold and numbing the extremities on this cold September morning. I wore my skull cap, covering both the ears. *Bugyal* was gleaming in the moonlight, aura was mesmerizing. Sunil showed us the final point to be reached before sunrise. A big cairn was visible at the ridge above. It was a steep ascent. We gradually kept the pace. I was really inspired by the courage shown by these girls. Their pace matched with young Sunil's. Even at times Sunil gave up the lead and one or the other lady would take over. Never ever did any of the ladies might have said about halting and taking rest.

We reached the *Sara Shakhare* (land of eighteen cairns) at 5:15 a.m. Wind had quelled a bit. I went to answer the nature's call mid way, for the catharsis is difficult to be commanded and I wonder how other guys manipulated their biological activities, for I never found any one moving away to do the same in whole sojourn. I was the only one who blatantly would ask for excuses to perform the same.

We pitched our tent and made a fire. Kerosene and dry twigs were carried along by us from the lower forest and before sunrise we had already captured the blissful landscape in our cameras. We performed our *Pooja* at first ray of Sun, and guzzled the local potion (*Moori*, apricot distillate) as *Prasad*, as per ritual, in makeshift hand cauldron, neat, after offering to almighty. I was the only tippler. We warmed our breakfast, prepared *Maggi* and had a sumptuous meal. At 8.00 am we broke the camp and headed toward *Kundi* top. Sky was cloudless, commanding beautiful view all around. We could appreciate the valleys along *Panvi Khad* leading all the way to *Shathul Pass* and *Chirgaon* (Rohru) region thereafter. Thispass, I along with Billu Wangpa had contemplated to cross over, this year, before the fall.

As we moved up the hill, big boulders broke the acceleration of girls. I found a strange kind of energy through this terrain and soon I was well up above them, communicating words of encouragement. Soon we were just 50 to 100 meters vertically below *Kundi* top, the highest point. We could appreciate the high peaks of *Bhaba* valley and *Sangla* valley. Also *Shrikhand* peak and *Kinner Kailash* ranges were also visible. *Pando Swar* and *Hans bastion*peaks were sprawling magnificently towards the east. I felt extreme excitement at the same time for I was lucky enough to appreciate the view of *Hans bastion* from opposite side (We had been to *Tia valley*, *Bhaba,* earlier), that also within 15 to 20 days.

Womenfolk didn't hike up to *Kundi* top, for we were directed by Sunil's Mom, that as per local custom a womanis not supposed to reach the top after *beesbhaado* (somewhere in first week of September) for the auspicious and pious time starts henceforth. The ladies respected the tradition and belief of local folk and enjoyed the view from lower altitude. I found a lot of *Brahma Kamal* and *Bhoot kesh* (wild, high alpine flowers) in this terrain.

I and Sunil explored the top to a bit too far. Wafting fog added to the serenity of this place. A big blue fish-shaped lake was visible toward *Bari Kanda*. We deciphered the pass towards *Rohru* region of District Shimla, though too far it was, above scree zone and blue glaciers. I wish we conquer it next year.

We spent almost one and half an hour on the top. Mobile signals were available but with a weak network. Around 11:30 a.m. we headed down. We had a grand lunch of *chapatis* and *sabzi*, just beneath the top on a wild green moor. As soon as we finished the meal, I picked up that strange headache. As we rested for some time after lunch I could feel the heaviness and nausea. The elevation was around 4500 meters, still I encountered that headache.

All the ladies seem fit. I tried to have a nap, for we were awake since yester midnight, but that nausea won't allow.

As we descended towards *Chhot kanda,* I couldn't enjoy the blissful view and mesmerizing aura overlooking *Bari* and *Nichar* valley simultaneously, with hide and seek played by intermittent fog. I had to take *aspirin* and within five minutes I felt all fresh.

Descent was much breathtaking than ascent. On the behest of Vijay, Sunil kept uprooting local *Jadi dhoop*, used as incense. I had neither the desire nor the strength to do the same. Ms. Bindu helped Sunil, even when she was also suffering from headache. Later she also took the magic pill, and all the worries were gone. It was only toward the end when I got to know that she is also a *Navodaya* alumnus, hence tough!

The vigor of girls was a bit lost but still they never lingered. We reached*Chhot Kanda* around 6:20 p.m. Total distance covered was 24 kilometers in 17.17 hours, courtesy my smart band, smart technology. Incredible journey it was indeed. We all were jubilant for we had vanquishing the beast, especially young ladies. These girls never gave up and seem fresh after reaching the base.

We were late by a couple of hours than scheduled time. Through the day I asked the girls to prepare dinner tonight at our own, for Sunil's family need not to be disturbed as his wife ought to look after their two kids. We had contemplated to pitch our tents in nearby field as the concluding night of the sojourn would be blissful under starry night and bon fire. Two people were supposed to make a fire while other two would prepare dinner.

By the time we reached Sunil's home, his spouse had already made dinner. We really felt down but her hospitality was much beyond explicitly. Sunil roasted dried lamb for night as we were the only two non-vegetarians. I and Sunil set up the tent and made a huge fire.

As we were enjoying the dinner, Sunil brought local, aged *Moori*. It was served by our female member. I was the only bibulous person in this whole lot. To alleviate the fatigue I gulped a couple of pegs down my throat and it really tasted awesome. At 9:30 p.m. we had gathered around huge fire. Though we didn't have enough energy to dance or sing, but appraised our day long journey.

At 11:30 p.m., after having green tea we went for sleep. I and Sunil occupied small *two men tent* and the ladies bigger one. As soon as I slipped inside my bag I was overpowered by deep slumber only to be awakened by a phone call. It was Vijay, who was calling as her younger sister was coughing uninterrupted. It was midnight and to move inside Sunil's house was not appropriate as the young kids must be resting. I suggested her to ransack my bag for it contained the first aid kit. I could hear the murmurs inside nearby tent. When did I again slip into slumber I never knew?

I got up at 6:15 a.m., everything was calm and cool. Outside it was bright sunny day again. We had a sumptuous breakfast at Sunil's home. I was told by Vijay that it was due to allergy that her sister suffered the cough which subsequently got right.

Sunil's kids accompanied us up to camping site. The sheer joy was visible on their faces as they rock and roll inside tents, ultimately ought to be goaded out. We thanked Sunil and his wife for their unmatched hospitality. Had it not been him, perhaps we would not have been able to circumnavigate the *Kundi Pabang* or perhaps not even reached up to *Sara Shakhare* at the first place. The late night start worked well and we could execute the plan perfectly.

At 8:15 a.m. we headed back from *Chhot Kanda* to *Nichar*. A strange sense of achievement prevailed and also the sense of oneness. In these last 36 hours we knew each other well, from being complete stranger earlier. This is what these journeys take you to. I appreciated the steel *Will* of these women folk and the sheer enthusiasm they showed throughout this journey.

Who says any work is masculine and can be categorized according to gender? No wonder had the patriarchal system been abolished long ago, who knows the first ascent of highest peak of the world would have been achieved by a woman!

Chantal Mouduit should be remembered for her love and infatuation towards mountains, not for her frolics and paraphilias as wrongly apprehended by many people including me!

To me, what I all gained in this sojourn is the confidence, that irrespective of gender; journey could be blissful if taken positively.

A strange sense of parting each other was pervaded as we reached *Nichar*. I saluted the budding zealous mountaineers while dispersing our own way. I wish we get a chance to explore some other valley soon, together. "*Ho..La..Se*"

Above the clouds, Kaangatey Dhaar, Bhaba-Lippa Pass, Kinnaur

Beauty of Barrenness, Below Bhaba-Lippa Pass, Kinnaur

Belnu Kanda, Taranda Valley, Kinnaur

Beautiful Mulling Pasture, Bhaba Valley, Kinnaur

Sara shakhare, Nichar

Manrangche, Bhaba Valley

Yula Temple

Huge old glaciers Below Lippa Khago, Kinnaur

At the top of Charang La, Kinnaur

Women as hiking partner, Kundi, Nichar Valley, Kinnaur

Mini Marathon, Rampur Bushahar, Shimla

Towering peaks with icefield, Bhaba-Lippa Pass Kinnaur

With Shepherds somewhere in Pin Valley, Billu Wangpa extreme left

Dried Mutton beads, Pin Valley, Spiti

At the top of Pin-Parvati Pass

Top: Shaathul Pass, Kinnaur

Manntalai glacial lakes, Parvati Valley, Kullu.

Scree Zone below Lippa Khago, Kinnaur

Serene camping site, Hamta Pass trek, Kullu to Lahaul

Valleys below Churdhar range, Sirmaur

Ethereal view from Kinnaur Kailash

Shepherds feeding guard dogs, the saviors

Beautiful trails above Dayara thach, Chandranahan, Rohru, Shimla

Chandernahan Lake, Chirgaon subdivision, Shimla

Melting glaciers, Tepong, Bhaba-Lippa top, Kinnaur

Running Soul

November 2019, Rampur Bushahar, HP

5.45 AM

Early November dawn, one can feel the constant pummels of cold breeze blowing sporadically. Not much movement appreciable at this hour. Outside, a few stray animals walking through the snarled lanes across highway. 24x7 *chaiwala* kiosk at the bus stop is also closed. As we drove through the National Highway-05, a few strangers we could find walking by the foot path, maybe to catch early bus to their destination. We are wearing jogging attire, above it warm zipper to parry away the cold. We saw one policeman abutting the cross road. We are very much excited, no words to manifest our exuberance.

It's a mini marathon being organized by the district administration to make people aware about drug menace. For the first time it's taking place in this part of the world in traditional *Lavi* fair at Rampur bushahar and here we are looking for the venue of this event.

As we walked around the mentioned venue we could find no one especially any running soul. Even the policeman was clueless about the event. After about 10 minutes, we found a group of youngsters with an elderly looking fellow walking past old bus station. I rolled down my car's window and inquired about event if any. To their surprise also they were here for participating in this marathon and had ransacked the whole arena in order to find venue without success. They couldn't find any sign board or placard around, indicating starting point. These were army personnel and the elderly looking guy was in charge. We were right in our guess while we watch the logo on the back of their track suits. Quite young athletic build, lean body, a zero haircut; they seem perfect guys to be at the podium. We felt much exasperated for no organizers, or their representative could be reached.

6.15 AM

With break of first light people started to pour at scheduled venue. A few youngsters, school, college goers moving around; some in groups, gossiping and a few seriously reticent. A few elderly looking, routine morning walker were also spotted passing by the starting venue guessing wildly for any function over there, that was about to take place withoutproper advertisement.

I heard about this event two months ago through an organizer friend and was really thrilled.

Trekking season was over for the year and I was complacent about my summer sojourns. Three treks have been accomplished successfully this year but still one cannot lie down lethargically for rest of the year as some strong physical activities were needed to keep the body well in shape for next season.

Jogging is my favorite work out. I always apprehend orgasmic bliss while steaming through the coldness of winter, sweat dripping through the brows. One doesn't need any special equipment for this sport. A pair of good running shoes is all that is needed. After my *Hamta* pass expedition all I left was with routine morning jogs. Soccer session at local football ground was not regular, for kids were busy with their exams and the amateur had lost the interest and motivation. A few soccer maniacs got transferred to other places hence I found playground empty most of the time.

After hearing the news about mini marathon, I had started to contemplate seriously about participating in this event. Though I jog routinely for a minimum of four to five kilometers and for once I did attempted ten kilometers but reached only up to eight, comfortably. But then these are jogs, slow jogs, not fast running that also in solitude not amid throng of a competition. I wanted to feel that competitive aura or those strange but lovely sensation that one encounter in any competition.

I won't be there just to participate but to give it a tough fight, I resolved. Had it been advertised in summer, would have got sufficient time to practice, I thought. But still 45 days were sufficient for thorough practice. Well I knew, it really doesn't matter mentally but physically changes over time cannot be ignored. I was in my late thirties and my beards had turned grey! Does that really matter, I pondered. My practice arena was big school play ground at *Duttnagar* (Rampur) or highway, at *Nigulsari* (Kinnaur).

I never tried to time my performance for I would be happy to complete this marathon irrespective of any time frame. During our childhood, back in village running was a mandatory part of daily life. Mum would be busy at field work whole morning only to reach back home late and then we would get ready to school. In order to reach there on time, it was a brisk run of two to three kilometers daily. The running etiquette got nourished further in boarding when I got a chance to participate in athletic meet at junior cluster level. Also we would see many seniors of school sticking to routine running session every morning and eventually brought some laurel when finally they bagged the prizes and thus got rewarded for their hard work. One becomes a hero in fraternity indeed. That motivated us youngsters to achieve something.

I still remember the moment when we were at *Sangli* Maharashtra to take part in cluster level sports and athletics event. I was there to participate in 800 meters run, for I was good in short distance running perhaps due to childhood errands. I met another participant from host school before the final event. I had always been oblivious about the minutes and statistical analyses of the training but he was kind of guy asking many questions from everyone about their performances, practice mode, previous best timings etc. He seems to me an excited piece of moron. I told him I never timed myself till date and all I knew, I can run fast. He was really surprised. "How come? You are to participate in a competition and you don't know your best?" I was representing Goa (*Canacona*). It was the year 1996 and I was 14 years old.

Once you are inside the competition arena, strange &inexplicable feelings starts to erupt involuntarily. I could hear the loudspeaker introducing the participants.

Toed to the line, positioned, get, set and go. I felt quite strong as l sailed past the other bunch within seconds. I could hear my name being mentioned over the loudspeaker as I was the lead runner. As I reached the last 100 meters my heart started to pound heavily, breath became shallow, a strange pain construed inside my gut and my thigh muscles started to shake involuntarily. This all happened within seconds but I could feel all this actually in slow motion. All my strength was gone. Just then the other lot got past me, the *Maharashtrian* leading the pack, his name being yelled over loudspeaker, crowd cheering up wildly. I finally crossed the finishing line limping, dejected with drooping shoulders. Later at dinner table I met the *Maharashtrian* guy, congratulate him for getting the gold. He consoled me with better luck next time and appreciated my efforts. "But that timing really matter" he advised.

Running all alone is a completely different proposition then to run in a herd. More so, if it is a competition, more thrill one find. So just to apprehend that orgy I was here at mini marathon. Though giving a whole hearted attempt was the motto. Also this kind of marathon was being organized for the maiden time in the annals of *Lavi* fair.

Almost two months ago, I reached the superintendent's office, the place where it was said that registration for the mini marathon would take place and asked as if I was at the right place for registration. The young hefty looking fellow on the other side of the desk nodded with broad smirk and looked toward another colleague sitting in one of the corner. He examined me top to toe and given my grey beards asked who will participate. I said me, raising my chest proudly. There were two categories actually; one for *under* nineteen age group (5 Kilometers) and other open (10 Kilometers). I further queried inquisitively that how much participant has registered as of now, to which he gingerly said, "You are the second one, first being me!"Was that an innuendo or reality, I wondered. It was the first day of registration and I wished more participation would come over time.

7:00 AM

Hustle and bustle has grown with the day. It's a clear sky. Small starting platform '*Chaudhari Adda*' is falling short to accommodate the participants. There is a situation of traffic jam on National Highway-05. Portable loudspeaker is being used. People are coming in groups from all directions. Organizers are finding it difficult to manage the throng. Chest numbers and t-shirts are being distributed. Organizers are giving the necessary instructions on loudspeaker. Mob is getting more euphoric and anxious. A few are here to grab the t-shirts as a souvenir and are blatantly vociferous about it, while a few are just warming up at the sidelines, oblivious about the ruckus and conundrum spewing around.

My eyes are surreptitiously looking for such serious athletes, a true contender. A few guys are warming up zealotly at one corner. One young girl stretching up with earphone plugged into her both ears, imbibed in her own world. Her attire seems completely like that of a seasoned runner, that we watch on television. Those army men that we met early morning are also stretching up individually; reticent, without showing any expression of happiness or anxiety on their face. Gala was to the extent that as young as Primary School goers were queuing up to get their chest numbers and as old as octogenarians were sprawling around. Organizers, including our dear friend, the local station house officer, were too much busy in managing the event, for the scheduled start time had already clocked and yet everything was not in order.

7:45 AM

Final whistle is blown and the event started with *under 19* contingent. Adrenaline has started to rush in the veins. Everyone seems restless. However a few stayed calm and focused. These are the professional lot, mostly the army men, who must have participated in many such events regularly. I also tried to be focused and kept reticent. My friend must have felt the adrenaline rush too.

During my preparation in past one month I not only focused on enhancing the stamina but also followed strict dietary schedule. It was a good combination of *carbs* and proteins. I also referred to some blogs about what to do just before a run and how to proceed during a competitive run, but all these readings proved more to be kind of literary things. Actual situation was yet to be perceived. I marked an army *Jawan* who looked potential contestant to win a prize. All I thought was to be with him or just to follow him throughout the run. I kept following his activities as he forced his way down to start line amid the throng and I also shouldered my way just behind him.

8 AM Sharp

For open participants whistle is blown and here we go.

The route meandered through the banks of river Sutlej, first along the left bank and then after crossing the '*Brow*' Victorian bridge to the right bank. In fact I thought about giving it a trial run two to three days before the actual competition, evaluating my stamina along with checking the time of my performance. But Iwas highly occupied with *Lavi* fair work thus couldn't find enough time to do the same. However reconnaissance of the route was already done. To me the hardest part seemingly was the gradual ascent of almost one to two kilometer just before the point of return, but this was all to be apprehended in reality.

As the race started, most of the participants excelled with all guns blazing. However I kept trailing the Army *Jawan* slowly and steadily. There were many participants who ran with the extreme of their power and were soon away from sight. The *Jawan* kept the peace steady and so did I. There was a kind of traffic jam on the narrow Victoria bridge as we made our way towards *Brow* suburb. As I jostled my way through the mob across bridge, *Jawan* has already taken the lead. Where my friends were, I never knew! There was no time to look back.

Road along *Brow* and *Jagatkhana* was filled with white t-shirts, young, old, boys, girls all alike. Awesome morning vista it was indeed. Many residents had come out to their balconies and were cheering up the participants. Only those, who must not have heard about this event; might have got surprised. However organizers with the help of Administration had sealed the entire road for traffic. Cold November morning had been turned into hot and humid aura; drenched bodies were sizzling with sweat.

There was a complete silence as runners were engrossed in their own thoughts, evaluating their strength or maybe reprimanding, damning themselves.

After about three kilometers from start point, I saw many kids jogging strenuously and a few limping painfully. The *Jawan* that I followed had become a distant figure as his pace remained constant and I was trotting with a bit slower pace, but found still enough strength to keep moving. A three to four kilometers jog that I performed every morning was enough to strengthen my convictions that up to five or six kilometers I can enjoy the race without a second thought. Participants of both categories had mingled on the way.

I threw behind many figures young and old, as I cruised past the snarled lanes of *jagatkhana*town. Then came the diversion point. *Jagatkhana* bridge was marked as turning point for five kilometers event (*under* 19 exclusively), whereas 10kilometers run would proceed toward *Chaati* village. Many participants who registered themselves for 10 Km run and found no strength to continue, turned toward finishing line after crossing this bridge, relinquishing the race in middle.

Here after the throng became thinner. Only serious participants were excelling through this path. I found many youngsters making their way towards the point of return which was about 2-3 Km ahead. Army *jawan* that I followed was nowhere to be seen. I spotted a teenager trying his way hard to keep ahead of me. Slowly I decreased the gap. At one point of time I thought about exceeding him but as I put forth the long strides, so did he. So for the moment, it became a two men contest, and in this way we both were excelling.

About one kilometer from the point of return, I found the first party running towards opposite direction. They were the real contenders, almost all Army *Jawans* from morning batch.

The gradually ascent had started and the loud heart throbbing sound was audible as if passerby can also hear it. I asked one of the guy coming back, how far the point of return was. He told me that it was just a few hundred meters away. Also he clapped for our efforts and said we had almost reached. In fact we all were admiring each other.

No other thoughts or worries come into your mind while you are running. All you can hear is the sound of your trotting feet and thudding hearts.

As I negotiated the ascent I could see a queue of organizers standing at the point of return and stamping the fore arm of every participant who reach there, verifying his/her arrival. As I reached closer I found a few well acquainted figures, most of them school teachers. One of them was a local physical education teacher as we have played many football games together. He hailed my efforts with utmost ecstasy as I forwarded my arm to get stamped. While I was turning back I asked him how many had reached before me, to which he yelled excitedly, "You are the first one with grey beards, Sir!" This was sufficient to feel light in this situation. That young teen boy was just in front of me, as I found extreme energy after reaching this point of return. All my quandaries about reaching this far were quelled hereupon.

The young chap's pace has downed a lot, perhaps motivation was lacking as many people had already shot back and the chances of a medal were nil. He must have dreamt about being on the podium like all others. I gave him a few words of encouragement as I told him to keep moving ahead. I met many participants, a few with grey beards, coming towards the point of return in opposite direction. I clapped for them and told they had almost reached.

It was a gradual descent all the way back. One may think about long swift strides in this kind of terrain but by this time body has given up. One may try hard but the pace wasdifficult to enhance. I kept young guy in front of me as if we were working as a team now.

Shortly we reached *Jagatkhana* bridge, only a few people crossing it by now. A few were still walking from *Brow* side.

Here we got stamped again. After crossing the bridge it was all steep ascent of few metres very much difficult to negotiate. Body has worn out by now and the young lad has taken the lead. For once I thought about surpassing him but had to give up as my muscles won't act as per my wishes.

I found my friends ambling gaily, gossiping just before the finish line. As they saw me they cheered me up. I was happy to see them, "Look boys, I made it!" I wished to say but the words would never come out. I only forwarded my arm to show the two stamps and exactly at 8:45 a.m. I crossed the finish line to be cheered by many participants and spectators, SHO *Sahib* taking the lead. I wasn't down all but yet completely exhausted. I performed some relaxing exercises before meeting the superintendent.

He told me that out of top ten runners, nine were Army personnel and one local college guy. The girl whom I saw stretching with those ear buds in the morning came up blazing all the way to finish line, all fresh. Ravi (SHO) further told that she is college Marathon champion.

Shortly the friends also joined us. We took some memorable *selfies* before proceeding to our routine *Lavi* fair work for it was the concluding day of *Horse Show* being organized by the state Animal Husbandry Department.

It was not about getting a position, but to stand up to my conviction that I can do it, be it I am 37 years old and it took 45 minutes to cover ten kilometers. I brushed my grey beards proudly as I met the whole *Lavi* fair staff welcoming us at the office gate.

Life is all about setting the goals and trying hard to get them.

After concluding the *Horse Show* on a successful note, by evening it was time to raise the toast at local guest house with superiors, colleagues and subordinate staff.

All were celebrating, of course for different reasons.

Bhaba-Pin-Parvati – I

An exploration across three districts, Two High Passes, one Non Conventional Shakara Khago (5100msl) and another dreaded Parvati Pass (5300 msl)

Summers were receding fast. Monsoon rains have poured till fortnight ago. A clear weather was observed for last many days, a perfect time to explore the Himalayas more. I had joined back at *Duttnagar*, Rampur Bushahar, lately and the hectic schedule kept me engrossed in professional and personal affairs with very little time to think about any coveted expedition. Moreover there was no message from my old hiking partner Billu Negi. Recently, numerous landslides, the massive one of course, especially in District Kinnaur, had jolted the spirit up to core. A lot many innocent lives were lost, many bodies never ever retrieved. Undoubtedly, nature revenge is in more savage manner. I was really shocked by the news of *Nigulsari* (Kinnaur) land slide in particular, for I served there and inhabited that place almost for past three years. But candidly, this specific region above National Highway; was really precarious and I shuddered while crossing it for the first time. Gradually the terrain became acquainted and fear was gone, yet I was always wary at this point. Because of scary media coverage many freelance wonderers had cancelled their trips to high Himalayas through

Kinnaur region. In fact at times I also got consolation messages that I got transferred back on time as if it's always safe elsewhere! How myopic human beings are at times. I was contemplating to decipher an itinerary towards *Rohru* (Shimla) region from Kinnaur either *via Shathul Pass* (Panvi Village in Kinnaur to Rohal Village in Chirgaon) or *Rupin Pass* (Sangla to Tangnu) before the higher peaks get laden with snow as Billu Wangpa was untraceable and our promised *Bhaba-Pin-Parvati* expedition was slipping away.

Before consulting another party for final expedition; I dropped a message to Billu Wangpa enquiring about status of our previously planned expedition with very little hope, as lately he was also busy with his personal affairs. Surprisingly, that evening, I received a reply to be ready for it in next four days.

All my ecstasies aroused to the limits. My body language changed considerably, sometimes even humming in oblivion. I asked my wife to keep my rucksack ready for she nowadays doesn't nurture any doubt about my plans and its execution henceforth.

We were to start the expedition from *Bhaba valley*, Kinnaur district on 25th of August 2021. I applied leave from higher authorities and asked for kind cooperation from colleagues back at work place. It will be I and Billu Wangpa only two member's small party, all the way alpine style.

25th August 2021

As I hauled my backpack through snarled lanes of *Rampur Bushahar*, mild drizzle welcomed at local bus station.

I boarded the very first bus to well acquainted beautiful hamlet *Kafnu* in Bhaba valley, where Billu Negi was waiting eagerly to start the much coveted expedition.

Weather was clear past *Jeori* (Last town before tribal district). We saw immense destruction caused by nature's fury at *Nigulsari*. It was terrifying indeed. I reached *Kafnu* by noon. Adrenaline rush started at the very beginning, down at *Homte* village, and stayed up to last motor able point as the transport that Negi has arranged was an old, worn out, fully laden tipper truck with a driver, who was high on dope and the road was bumpy and narrow. Even Billu Negi was dumbstruck when the driver offered him his seat *en-route* with so much complacency as if it was just about holding to the wheel. We both watched each other's face stoically.

At *Karra* (High altitude pasture), our arrival was highly anticipated. When we reached there around 5 PM, farm guys (Govt. Sheep Breeding Farm, Kaksthal, Kinnaur) were busy in boiling mutton soup. A hot tea was served immediately. We had a brief gala enjoying local potion and mutton curry before retiring for the day. While resting inside my tent with the pounding heart I was thinking only about this ongoing expedition, where no one including Billu wangpa has ventured before.

26th August 2021

Next morning, we assessed our provision and kept busy in arranging backpacks. Expected numbers of days were 7 or maximum of 8. I had already packed my rucksack previous day, and its weight was damn good. Billu Negi handed over to me some more items. So now it must be around 40/45 pounds, though less than Billu wangpa's. We checked the working status of our round Kerosene stove which was just fine and loaded 3 liters of Kerosene oil, expectedly sufficient enough to thrive for that many days. Luckily the contractor of our high alpine pasture camp at Karra, Mr. Parmar was on his way up to *Chhotungrang* (a lush green pasture towards Shakara Pass) to bring some luggage on his draft animals. He offered the services of his mule for carrying our load up to that place, which we accepted eagerly. The only problem with Parmar was that he kept inebriated most of the time. By the time we started the final sojourn around 11.50 am, he was already teetering. We bade farewell to *Karra* and Billu Negi took the lead at times balancing Parmar and his ride, a poor but obedient mule. Spiti horses are really faithful animals. It was quite astonishing to see how they took him carefully through the narrow precarious unbridled path, amid sharp outcrops. I envied him, for I should have been rearing a thorough bred.

At *Chhotungrang,* local shepherd offered us glass of goat milk while Parmar unloaded our rucksack. We met some young boys, buzy in playing cards, who were also on their way to *Kheer Ganga*, though planning to take shortest route as per *Google Map*, by-passing the Shakara Khago, the conventional route. These young kids took mountaineering so lightly. Their backpack seems ill equipped and so were their convictions. We decided to set our camping time at 5.00 pm wherever we could find the suitable place to pitch the tent. As the kids excelled further, we stopped near a glacial stream, a fine camping site below *Wangshaangling* meadows.

After savoring dinner, we sat outside the tent. It was a star lit night and a strong feeling crept deep within as if we were approaching the sky gradually! After having a final bout of coffee under numerous galaxies, we slipped inside our sleeping bags around 9pm. Sleep is a temporary death and the dreams, new life.

27TH August 2021

It was a bright fog free morning. We got up around 6 in the morning. High peaks in our backdrop were glistening gold for the first ray of early morning sun had already kissed the beauty. We were camping prudently, a bit higher towards *Wangshaangling*, the last meadows beneath *Shakara* Pass. We had planned to cross the pass tomorrow and for the day we're to ascend as much higher as possible to set high advance base camp.

Weather was perfectly calm, only screeches of yellow billed Chugs were audible intermittently. We saw a big rat running frantically between huge boulders. As we broke the camp and proceeded further, the bottleneck was to cross the thudding stream, for the glacier above it was precarious and broken to great extent. Last year, Billu Wangpa and his small expedition party crossed it without much trouble.

Before Billu Negi tried to explore it, we had our fill with *Maggi*, left over *Dal-Rice* and *Masala* tea. Also we filled our thermos with extra tea to be consumed later in the day.

It was a testing day, the very first day to assess the actual endurance for whole expedition. It was a steep careful probe for Negi. He arduously muscled his way up the glacier as I busied myself shooting this incident. There was a huge crevasse across the glacier, which he found widening further. Towards the end, it was in the form of a slender bridge which could give way at any point of time. I yelled with the top of my voice and whistled, for the deafening sound of gushing stream would not let him hear my concern. After few moments he fortunately turned around. There is a narrow gray area between bravery and foolishness.

Soon we found a suitable place to cross over the stream. Billu, as usual took the lead. 'If he is immersed up to his haunches, how much shall I?' I dithered merely by its thought. But then we don't have any other options in such terrain. I pulled up my trousers up to knees, hung shoes over my shoulders and gradually anchored my sole in boulder strewn stream. At the middle of torrent, I was submerged up to my abdomen and the sheer force of gushing water was possessed to take me along. Billu wangpa's words of encouragement meant a lot in this moment. The first major river crossing was done gallantly. We celebrated new life puffing at the other bank of river, for there is always a thin line between life and death while crossing high Himalayan streams. After two hillocks and a wide glacier we reached a glade, overlooking *Wangshaangling* meadows.

"Wangshaangling is the base camp for Shakara Khago. It literally means 'Chain' in local dialect. A glacial stream bifurcate the highly fertile meadow in serpentine motion,

like a necklace. Shepherds from Bhaba and Rupi valley set up temporary camps here, before moving towards Pin valley. A few glaciers are visible around, hanging from sky scraping peaks. Only rock hard hikers should venture in this valley"; was my diary note for the day.

As we walked past *Wangshaangling*, a mild drizzle started. While Billu Wangpa was galloping ahead, I could feel the straps of my backpack biting into my shoulders. Perhaps it wasn't loaded appropriately; after all packing a rucksack is a hard learnt art. In a wide cave we unloaded our haul and it was time for lunch. Bread, fruit Jam, tea and biscuits proved energy enhancer. For now it was just one o'clock, and the weather had cleared up. We captured the ethereal view in our cameras and decided to give it a little push towards the Pass. Soon, fog started to swath the aura and cold wind picked up. It's not unusual how quickly the weather take turns at such altitudes. It was a steep ascent amid scree zone. We marked a small knoll, just beneath a brownish peak up above, where we shall explore some water body and find little flat surface to pitch the tent. The rain only increased with time and we would have literally been frozen, had we stopped progressing. We had to take shelter below big boulders almost for an hour till the rain mellowed down. As we were done with pitching the tent, weather finally cleared up. Sun rays illuminated the valleys down and innumerable high serrated peaks, all striped white, erupted in the sky eastward. Huge old glaciers were pervading over the *Kamba-Rupi* Pass south ward and just above our camp we saw nothing but moraine. The view was such magnetic that we left the whole work and sat quietly for a few minutes. In Billu Wangpa's words, *'the true happiness comes only after great sorrows.'*

We prepared our dinner over *Kero*-stove, under big rock which was finished well by 6 o'clock. Elevation was 4700msl. We relished the meals by 7pm with setting twilight, appreciating the blissful view and retired for the day at 8.30 pm.

28th August 2021

Around 6.30 am, I crept out of my sleeping bag, unzipped our tent, to witness a splendid morning view. Everything around was crystal clear. Very few clouds were at horizon towards west, but mild fog was wafting in the valleys down. Serrated barren peaks towards the east were spreading its magic around. The first thought that ran through my mind was to prepare breakfast before the drizzle starts. It had turned to be our routine ceremony as I would pump and light *Kero* stove, while Billu wangpa brought the fresh potable water from nearby stream. Regarding glacial water one thing is common, that in the afternoon all streams get muddled with soil and turn turbid, however in the morning due to freezing, only clear streak of water is witnessed, hence appropriate time to collect the water.

This was our summit day and we already had covered half the elevation previous day. As per Billu wangpa two more hours will lead us to *Shakara Pass*. Luckily it didn't drizzle and as we finally broke the camp around 9 am, fog started to parry away. I had recovered from my neck pain due to strap issue yesterday and vowed to buy a new branded rucksack next season. We ascended the moraine gradually, gazing the beautiful terrain and vast glaciers around. And then came the big sprawling ice ground just before the pass. We had to traverse it in order to reach the *Khago*. I was scared to extreme, for I had always been terrified walking over ice. But here was no second option. I took the lead, for the glacier was a bit flat initially. Again, Billu Wangpa motivated me with his signature thumbs up. After a few minutes we were across the glacier. But there wasn't defined trail towards top. All we could find was fragile, glacier minced rocks and scree, difficult to clamb. Billu wangpa adroitly ascended through a small muddy gully keeping each foot cautiously one behind another. I tried to emulate him but his footsteps had further aggravated the precarious trail. I had to turn back and find another route. At one point, I rested my rucksack and using all my limbs tried to explore the terrain. It was really dangerous, one small mistake and I would fall 300 meters straight down over hard ice field and may further skid off. I kept my eyes over the rock only, and yelled and whistled, but got no response from Billu. Was he alright? How would I proceed further? What if I fell down? How to get back? These questions were rapidly rippling through my mind. In such situations it becomes one on one. You have to be only yours peer. I was missing the most essential equipment, the rope. I turned down to the base, wore my helmet and tried to follow the gully that Billu Negi had ascended earlier. It was a bit safer than the more exposed out crop that I had *rekkied*. After a few meters, I could find more firm ground to clamber upon, a few rapid strides and *voila*...I was standing on the pass, a small crest. I supplicated to the almighty, bowed in front of hercules Mountain and felt how miniscule we are in front of mother nature. Billu wangpa was coming from other end. He had covered the whole crest in order to help me for he thought I must have taken another route. He even couldn't hear my whistles or cries. We performed a little *Pooja* by burning juniper shrubs that he collected down the valley. We ate dry fruits while appreciating the top view. Dark brownish *Spiti* valleys pervaded ahead. Gale was high and so was my headache, yes altitude sickness it was, for the pass stood at 5200msl. With the help of binoculars we tried to decipher our route down *Pin* valley and then intersection towards *Parvati* valley. We found a flock far down the *Pin* valley, our only hope, for even Billu Wangpa hasn't wandered through this terrain. After a brief rest of almost 30 minutes we descended carefully through boulders and scree. Billu Wangpa galloped ahead and I was wobbling behind. My neck pain has started again. The sun shone in cruelest manner. Along the stream, somewhere my walking pole got struck between boulders and bent abruptly. I was literally pushing each step. Billu wangpa never stopped and never looked back! 'Apna-apna'. Only at the designated point we had our lunch near a fresh water stream. I had to take aspirin. It must have been almost a couple of hours walk amid boulders and pebbles. I gobbled a few loaves of bread forcefully down my throat along with tea. The pass took every calorie out of our body and that half an hour duel was worth taking life. After a brief rest we started ahead and soon met a shepherd from *Rupi* valley, an acquaintance of Billu. We shared the pipe and talked about perspective of reaching the *Parvati* base as soon as possible. He suggested taking rest today at his *dera* down the valley, and tomorrow he will show us the route to the base. I asked him one question, how far his *dera* was.'Just half an hour straight walk', he told. It was morale booster indeed. We swung our rucksack and moved on. Billu Wangpa's pace never receded, and my gaze was constantly on wrist watch. Two hours had gone by, and there was sign of either Billu or the shepherd's hovel! At one point of time I couldn't see trail ahead as the land slide had devoured the entire arena down to gushing Pin river. I remembered almighty. As shepherd had told us that he will also tend his livestock to his *dera* by evening, I had to wait for him. By 5pm I could watch him goading his animals towards my direction, elated I was. "Half an hour"..., I wondered. After one more hour we finally reached the *dera*, Billu wangpa's Coleman tent laid beautifully outside. I was happy that I finally made it, and angry at the same time, for Billu Wangpa should have waited for me. I had decided, to say this expedition a goodbye, we won't be able to make it together, for the clear lack of communication it was. Billu Wangpa was busy in making mutton curry inside shepherd's hovel. He told that he waited for me and then decided to move on and get the tent pitched on time. I was in no mood to buy his arguments. Rather I rested in my tent contemplating to head towards *Mudh* all alone tomorrow, for instead of being one-on-one, it was better to reach safely back home, complacent with one high pass crossing, jeopardizing Wangpa's plan for the time being. I got up late in the evening only. Headache was gone and so was the tiredness. We had grand feast of dried meat inside shepherd's hovel. I slept alone in our tent as Billu decided to sleep with shepherds.

There is something about mountains that moves the soul. They arouse a powerful sense of spiritual feelings and a notion of our own life being ephemeral and mortally fragile. It denotes our insignificant place in the universe. They have about them an ethereal, evocative addiction that I found impossible to resist.

Bhaba-Pin-Parvati – II

After successful ascent of *Shakara* Pass, due to sheer fatigue and mis-communications thereafter, I was resolute to turn towards *Mudh* village curtailing the proposed *Pin-Parvati* Pass expedition in the middle, till last night. However, new morning brought new hope and we paired up again with rejuvenated ecstasies and vigor.

29th August 2021

I was feeling damn fresh today. With cool mind I thought, if I decide to abort this expedition, it would jeopardize Billu Wangpa's aspirations also. I wouldn't be able to make it next time as well. At least with Billu, somehow I can drag on. I decided to carry on.

But before moving ahead I told him candidly that we have to move together, he matching mine pace, to which he agreed instantly.

Again Bittu *Aate* and his shepherd partner, who might be in his sixties given the creases on his sun tanned face, showed their benevolence and prepared lavish brunch of mix *Daal*, rice and sheep's lard. Hot tea was filled in the thermos and six *chappatis* packed separately, to be consumed mid way. Before bidding adieu they offered us dried mutton from the beads lying outside in the bright sun, which we accepted humbly. It would be a grand feast once we accomplish *Pin-Parvati* pass. My watch struck 10 AM when we finally departed. Bittu Aate showed the shortest way towards Parvati base, which would take six hours to reach there. 'Six hours'. I giggled, multiplied by two!

We were to reach up to confluence of two small rivulets in *Spiti* valley; a beautiful routine camping site for traditional *Bhaba-Pin* pass, called *Mangrangche*, and then take left turn without crossing the bridge. It was the shortest route suggested by the shepherd.

The trail was shaky, as loose gravel and big boulders embellished the whole terrain and I felt as if it will go on like this till eternity along muddy torrent downwards.

Today, we both walked in sync as I followed Wangpa. We had intermittent breaks and brief talks. We both were concerned about the unknown perilous trail. I felt rather comfortable today. Mutual understanding was developing fast between us. We saw the first glacier up the valley across gushing stream and kept negotiating the big rock strewn terrain all around; keeping foot one after another cautiously, for a small recklessness would have been certainly fatal. We didn't exchange a word, when necessary sign and body language was enough. All we heard was the familiar clinks of the metal tip of our walking pole hitting against the rock. We traversed the first glacier, with the hope that the second would come soon for we were supposed to cross it in order to reach the actual trail visible on the other side of river. We saw some trekkers coming through this wide trail, torpor to the extent suggesting it must have been a hard time crossing *Pin Parvati* pass. We waived at each other, words not exchanged, as the roaring river was calling the shots. At one highly perched knoll, in an abandoned shepherd's *dera*, we finally sat to relish the lunch. It was past noon and the second glacier was visible at far end of the valley.

Crossing this glacier was the frightening moment of the day. There were no defined footholds of any kind to scale nearly ninety degree wall of loose gravel and sandy soil. Billu Wangpa showed his inborn skills to reach the top after putting all his limbs to work. I could merely watch him progressing upwards and shuddered with the prospect. One drop and you surely get hit hard on cold ice, or who knows slid all the way to big crevasse down. I remembered almighty. Without letting my mind divert, I used my whole body parts to clamber up the wall, not having a glance down mid way. Billu Wangpa could only watch me helplessly from above. We again missed the rope a lot indeed. Once on the top, it was a victory to be cherished, may be more than conquering the pass itself! 'To hell with it', I mumbled quietly while puffing the pipe. We wondered how the flocks of sheep and goat had crossed the river over this glacier, but then at such terrain topography might have change in no time.

Two more small streams were crossed and it was time to look for appropriate place to pitch the tent as scheduled 5 o'clock time had reached.

We had made it a rule since the very first day of our expedition that come what may, by 5 pm we would start the search for camping site, by 6pm we would set the camp and by 7 our dinner must be ready before dark. But as per shepherds we must be close to *Parvati* base. We agreed to keep our pace for next half an hour. It was a gentle grade along fierce stream, but the trail seems unending. Also some clouds had gathered towards the horizon in the direction of the Pass. And there we saw that beautiful glade just beneath snow capped huge mountains sprawling across quiet rivulet. This was the *Parvati* base camping site. We literally rushed to reach there before a downpour hit us. Fog had swathed the aura. We saw four small tents pitched there. Before enquiring anything, we quickly pitched the tent as drizzle turned into heavy rain.

That evening we used our poncho to prepare a makeshift kitchen outside our tent. By early night, weather had cleared up and starry night was just awesome.

Tomorrow, was designated our rest day. We enjoyed our routine night coffee under open sky and it was indeed a hard day spent.

30th August 2021

Next morning we got to know that it was a trekking group coming down from *Parvati* Pass, clientele a Bengali couple. '*If they could make it, so would I*', I thought. We took first hand information from them about route, bottlenecks etc. They said goodbye around half past nine and descended towards *Mudh*. The whole *Parvati* base was left to us and to some yellow billed Chugs.

After breakfast, basking in bright sun, Billu came up with a brisk straight question. "Why do you wander in the mountains, Sir"? I thought for a few moments and replied, "Actually I want to find solace, and to feel the hardships; to get over it, to know more of myself and all this of course because of motivation I get from adventure books". "And why you"? I asked. "Sir I feel alive in the mountains, it is just like finding the true meaning of life". Billu answered. Different reasons but same perspective.

We cancelled the plan of resting and decided to explore the trail towards the pass same day, so that assault would be easy next morning.

We proceeded around noon. For our surprise, nobody told us about this upcoming ordeal as we had to cross the river half an hour later. The flow was fierce and the water reached over Billu's waist who as always took the customary lead with his twin staves. I followed remembering almighty. Crossing river successfully is always like gaining a new life. Thereupon it was a straight climb all the way. While the altitude was rising, we followed a rhythm, a few steps and rest. Billu Wangpa was complaining headache today, but I felt fresh, at times taking the lead. By 3pm, we could watch the base far below us. After crossing a couple of streams, which changed colour from transparent to brown gradually, in front of our eyes, we found a plain area to pitch the tent. We prepared food by 5pm as the wind picked up hereupon, and temperature plummeted much below. It was a huge glacier above us and the icy wind won't let us enjoy the evening view. Suddenly I suffered from that altitude headache too and soon after dinner I got zipped inside our sleeping bags. It was 6pm only. Fortunately no rainfall occurred that night and the winds were gone by morning along with the headache.

31st August 2021

I woke up to still weather around 6.00 am. Sleep was shaky, for the intermittent fluttering of tarpaulin tent against fierce wind broke the slumber and comparatively thin air at 4900 meters altitude isn't a suitable place for it. Sky was cloudless. All headache and fatigue was gone. Sun rose quite early as we were camping on the east face of mountain. Routine cooking schedule followed, I lighting the stove and Billu Wangpa collecting potable water from nearby stream which by now were frozen to mere trickle. Tea, soup, *Maggi*, evening's left over, were relished as breakfast and utensils washed before breaking the camp. We were excited about the Pass. As per hikers at base camp it would take just an hour to reach the same, I considered that two.

At 9 o'clock we finally made the ultimate assault. The rhythmic advancement was mandatory now. Billu Wangpa excelled ahead with his reconnoiter eyes and I followed him gradually. After climbing a small hillock, it was a huge snow field all around. Generally the travelers mark the pass with *chortens* and flags, but we couldn't appreciate any. There were two possible passes, one towards east and another towards west. And to get lost at such altitudes is almost fatal. Billu Wangpa checked for his offline map showing direction to eastwards. We had to scale a giant old glacier of blue ice with huge crevasses in the middle. Here our binoculars proved its essentiality. We got a hint of small fluttering flag towards east at the left top of glacier and started to move in this direction. I made a small video en route. Wangpa trotted the ice like Spiti horse, being wary about each crevasse while I tried to keep myself on his footprints. After half an hour of climb, that weird headache started to develop. I felt damn thirsty. At one point of time I threw my rucksack over ice and sat upon it. I wanted to be still. I whistled to Billu and signaled him to bring water, for my bottle was empty. He came down with the bottle and the news that we were almost at the pass. I soaked my throat, and by putting all strength together, hauled my load towards the pass. Soon I could see the cairns and prayer flags fluttering calmly. 5300 meters… woaw, we made it finally.

It was mesmerizing view from the top. Here were beautiful glaciers all around each bigger than other. I haven't seen such a blissful pass and the panoramic view ever. We hugged each other raised our arms and paid our obeisance to Mother Nature. It was eleven o'clock.

We stayed there for almost 20 to 25 minutes and decided to descend, for my headache has only intensified. High altitude sickness, it was. Carefully we negotiated the other side of pass which was the lip of another big glacier with possibly numerous crevasses. I was literally limping, for the headache and the fatigue was unprecedented. Billu Wangpa's gadget was working well and his sixth sense of finding the right trail was automatically activated. Had he taken the left, easier looking route past 'brown mountain' we would have reached no where except those dreaded *Maan Talai* glacial lakes. Again it was a small ascent past this mountain. I sat down exasperated while Billu wangpa vanished ahead to explore the terrain. After five minutes he appeared back and I asked him sullenly what lies ahead. "All ice Sir", he replied curtly. "May be further down we could see some valley". He understood my situation, though he later admitted that he was feeling the same, and we decided to take a coffee break. Biscuits, bread-jam and coffee. It proved beneficial. Still that headache was the big issue. We started to descend down the glacier after an hour of rest. As we kept moving down gradually, we could see some dry terrain and some camping sites far below. We were on the right track. It bolstered our morale. As we lost the altitude slowly my headache was turning mild. Sooner we found that routine trail amid boulders and scree with intermittent cairns erected as landmarks. After crossing a muddy stream we reached the 'view point' as per map, from where an ethereal view of numerous glacial lakes of *Maan Talai* could be seen. It was a unique view indeed. After an hour we were slowly jogging across *Maan Talai* plains.

Maan Talai is a huge basin for glacier fed *Parvati*river, which get inundated during monsoon and turn into a vast lake. But at this moment it was just like a fine meadow, though we didn't found any shepherd or trekker that day. By 5pm, our feast of dried mutton gifted by *Rupi* Shepherds was being roasted inside a temporary hovel left by the retreating shepherds. What else could be the best occasion to celebrate our successful ascent and that also when whole *Man Talai* was only to us?

Azure sky, beautiful snow capped peaks shrouded in wafting fog and utmost serenity added to the celebration of this victory.

1st September 2021

It was all white outside when we woke up. It snowed all night, while we slept soundly in complete exhaustion. Had we camped a bit higher, we would have been in big trouble. It was just a mesmerizing view and we sang in unison only to be witnessed by barren rocks. Slowly the weather cleared. We packed up around 9.00 am. We were disheartened to watch the heap of trash all around at such a beautiful place. We performed a small *Pooja* at *Man Talai* temple, an open place, with tridents of various sizes erected here by the devotees. The beautiful peaks in the backdrop symbolize Lord Shiva and Maa Parvati.

We hurried towards *Odi thaach*, where we met some Nepali porters coming down from another high pass (*Dhabaas Pass*) in Pin valley with Bengali trekkers. They ought to camp high last night amid snow storm. We wondered how people explore extreme locations. We noted down their contacts. "May be next time", Billu told them. From *Odi thaach* to *Pandu Pul*, it's a straight walk. At *Pandu pul* we lost the trek. Instead of crossing the natural bridge of big boulders leftward; we kept walking straightahead, for the thick canopy hid the miniscule trail. We were tired and one shepherd showed us an alternate route. But instead of going down, the trail took us upward. The dusk was setting and we couldn't find any suitable place to pitch the tent. I cursed the poor shepherd.

We could see the usual trail on the other bank of river. Weather took its turn and the fog started to fill the arena. Visibility went down to bare minimum. I couldn't see Billu Wangpa. It was a perfect situation to get lost. I could find some fresh pellets of sheep and goat, hoping that a flock must be around. Soon I heard the bleating of livestock with Billu Wangpa talking to herdsman. That night we were the guest of these nomads, local Kullu shepherds, we even cooked inside their small shed. For the first time in past eight days we heard about outside world, thank to small radio set owned by the shepherds.

2nd September 2021

Nothing is certain in this terrain. It rained throughout nigh. Next morning as weather cleared gradually, I found that we were camping at a perfect site. The normal trail was sprawling to the other side of river much below us. We must have scaled almost 800 meters last evening. We departed only after relishing a great feast of fried potatoes with *chappatis*. *Chappatis* after 8 days!

An old shepherd, who was not feeling well, accompanied us towards *Kheer Ganga* and further to his home place at Kullu. Health facilities are the biggest worry at such places for even the first aid could be sought only after walking for miles. We had to cross a *jhulla* on *Parvati*river in order to reach the traditional trail, but as Billu wangpa muscled the old man across river and returned to lift me, the small basket came off the cable. There was no one else to help us. It took us almost a couple of hours to fix the issue, and moved ahead, exhausted completely. And then we encountered the rock climb near *Tunda Bhuj*. A huge barrel shaped rock had to be negotiated with the help of a fixed rope, which seems worn out. Roaring river*Parvati* was flowing menacingly below this rocky terrain. If someone slip accidentally down, it was certain that even the body could never be retrieved. The path was so precarious that even goats could not cross past it. So the flocks were kept upstream on the other bank of river with the hope that snowing in upper reaches will mellow the water level and the flocks may cross it henceforth. Billu wangpa checked the strength of the rope and abseiled down. He could sniff the danger. Slowly, he belayed down the rock, with utmost precision. Then I dispatched the old sick shepherd, who was so much scared that it took few minutes to placate him. And then with the words of constant encouragement from Billu wangpa, I climbed down the rock. Here my climbing helmet proved its worth.

Hereafter trail was gradually gentle and we reached the tree line of *Tunda Bhuj*. Trees after nine days!

Tunda Bhuj, a charismatic glade which may entice anyone, made me to hum a song, *into the heaven……*

At nearby stream, we enjoyed a brief tea – biscuit-bread-*channa* (baked gram) and chocolates. Now the trail undulate down through fir and rhododendron thick forest and then after walking for almost two hours, suddenly a mottled place of land appeared in front of our eyes. Numerous colored tarpaulin tents were erected here and loud noises were heard intermittently. We have just reached to an extreme society, from sheer hard life to all luxury filled gala, how quickly the transition took! We had planned to pitch the tent that night as well but the paucity of time, constant drizzle and lack of space didn't allowed us to fulfill our plan. We booked a room in temple rest house, had a simple dinner before sleep enveloped us amid the late night din of rave party?

3rd September 2021

Rain was persistent all through night, as if it was just waiting for our expedition to be concluded. It was local deity's *pooja* here, today. *Kheer Ganga* would witness annual congregation of local devotees. By the time we left the bed, old shepherd, Prem Singh had arrived back after taking hot sulfur shower, looking all fresh. Hot spring beside an old temple is the main attraction of *Kheer Ganga*. He was in a hurry to get back to his home for the local bus ought to be caught well on time at *Bhuntar.* We promised to keep in touch, exchanged contacts, and who knows we shall meet at *Chander Tal* lake in Lahaul where his flock will graze next summer! We paid our obeisance at temple after taking hot water bath, which was refreshing indeed. A thorough bath after nine days! All fatigue was gone instantly. *Kheer Ganga* not only has religious connotation but a heaven for hippies who want to get high on weed and night parties. For now the season was almost gone and most of the shacks were looking empty. Earlier it used to be a secluded place away from town's bustle, amid nature's beauty replete with foreign tourists. But nowadays it's all about indigenous tourists.

At around 10 am we started to descend all the way down to *Bershaini*, last motor able point, a three hours hike down the lush green valley. A feeling of conquest prevailed. People including local devotees and tourists were ambling in the opposite direction. Someone asked inquisitively given our condition, equipments and perhaps exuberance, whether we were coming from Pin valley, to which I smirked and replied "Yes, but only after crossing *Bhaba* valley, Kinnaur."

At around noon we saw the hydro electric project site and the road beside *Parvati* river. We found mobile signal just above *Bershaini* and after 9 days contacted back home. There was hue and cry there, for I told them I will be off signal for four to five days. They were about to lodge missing report today!

From *Bershaini* we gazed the valley upward and wondered how we traversed all the way from *Bhaba* valley (Kinnaur) to *Pin valley* (Lahaul Spiti) and then to *Parvati valley* (Kullu). It was a circuit of more than hundreds of kilometers, completed finally in 10 days, thankfully just in a single piece!

We again congratulated each other, a strange feeling of brotherhood erupted, but the expedition was not over yet. A grand celebration was highly deserved at Kullu town.

A lot many places were explored during this expedition, transient terrain including two 5000 plus passes, myriad river crossings, met different people and saw the end moments closely at various occasions. But the best thing was we explored ourselves more than anything else.

The Guided Trek, Hamta Pass

2018

We had already heard a lot about Pin-Parvati Pass, from friends and some arduous trekkers, though I was having little knowledge of the exact terrains and the level of hike one needs to undergo. But I was very much excited to give it a try along with some close hiking partners. All we knew were that it will take at least one week to cross the pass. On enquiring from some Kinnaur guides, we were told that most of the guided treks in that region are organized and executed by Manali people.

One contact was shared and I dialed it inquisitively.

Hira bhai was a professional guide at Manali. A Kulluvi localite, his demeanor and dialect confirmed about his personality. A simple, sober guy full with positive energy; was his hallmark, at least what I could assess from the small talk we had about Pin-Parvati Trek. He was ready to guide us through it with the paltry sum of wages on daily basis.

I explained my plans among hiking partners, but surprisingly this time all of them were reluctant. May be the number of days required were too much or the dreaded stories of big crevasses across the massive glacier en-route might have dithered them, ultimately aborting the expedition.

I explained the things to Hira bhai over phone and requested him if I could be accommodated with any group being guided towards Pin-Parvati Pass this season.

After a few days he called me back and told, for now no clients were available to the arduous Pin-Parvati trek but a group of foreigners was to ascend Hamta Pass in Manali, next week. He invited me to join the same which I accepted eagerly. Candidly I had no know-how either about Manali or the Passes around it. However a friend of mine told me that Hamta was a picturesque Pass between Kullu and Lahaul valley.

I had never ever joined any guided trek till now and it was a perfect opportunity to apprehend such expedition from close quarters.

It was the month of July 2018. After having verbal spat with family, as always expected before any expedition, I boarded first bus to Kullu. Around *Luhri*, mild drizzle started leading to frequent calls from home, though it didn't shattered my resolution. Terrain past *Jalori* Pass was awesome as always. Magnificent valleys down *Jibhi* and *Sojha* were as attractive as ever, enticing every tourist at its best. I reached Kullu around 4 PM. Humidity was as usual, but the sky had cleared by now.

I took the bus to Manali as one of my friends was waiting for me there. At around 6 o'clock, I reached Manali. Weather was cool and perfect, no sign of rain.

The much boasted Mall road was abuzz with numerous tourists, like always. I preferred to saunter around a bit and purchased essentials before calling my friend.

By evening, I called Hira bhai and told him about my arrival. He seems anxious to meet, as rest of the trekkers had also reached Manali. I was all in excitement whole night, for I neither knew the guides nor the clients.

Next morning I got a call from Hira bhai. It must be 7 am. I thought it was regarding timings and place to meet but in fact there was a bad news. A casualty happened in his family back in village last night and he had to curtail his expedition suddenly. Before I could figure out what will happen to me, his mellow voice assured that the expedition would proceed as per plan, except his cousin Sanjeev taking over the head guide's role. He was supposed to call me sooner. A strange town, strange pass, strange trekkers and now strange guide! Was it exhilaration or exasperation, I never knew.

I had a lavish breakfast with my friend, who accompanied me up to much acclaimed *Prini* village (home of ex-Prime Minister, Late Sh. AB Vajpayee), the point of rendezvous. We waited and waited. A diversion towards Hamta Village lies ahead. Had it not been Nitin (my friend), I would have started to scale the path, for it was past noon and no contact could be established with Sanjeev. Usual traffic plied over not-so-busy road, until a rugged, utility cab, spewing loud noise, approached us with furious speed and took a U-turn in front of our eyes.

It stopped abruptly with screeching sound of ungreased breaks. Thanks to my huge rucksack that they made up their mind that the only trekker left must be me. Open trunk of the cab was loaded with many backpacks, cooking utensils, raw food materials and camping gears.

One small head came out through partly rolled down window pane and enquired whether I was the guy? As I nodded, the door was slightly opened and I ushered into the cab's hind cabin, locating my seat with utmost difficulty. There were 8-9 passengers already inside it, no one with foreign appearance. I hesitantly quibbled, 'Mr Sanjeev?'

A man in his thirties with round hat, well trimmed moustache, tanned face sporting black shades, turned around and grinned at me. A nice head guide's appearance, I thought. Most of the co-passengers were teens apparently and beaming with excitement. Thankfully I could understand their dialect a bit thus not feeling uncomfortable at all.

Later I was told that the foreign clients had already departed in a different cab ahead of us up to last motor able point.

Hamta is a small hamlet located amid rhododendron and fir trees much above *Prini* village, houses built in old fashion, slated roofs. The *kutcha* road that led us to this village had many switch backs, cab bumping frequently and so do the passengers, like pop corns.

As we got down from the vehicle at last point, I saw a big water body below this place. It was dam site reservoir to feed a hydropower station down the valley. After walking for few minutes, I saw the trekkers wandering around a small *dhaba*, a few busy with photography and a few with pipes.

All were Malaysian.

They were being briefed by a lanky young man, wearing pea cap; later I found another guide Mr. Naresh Sharma. As I weretrying to hear the conversation, Sanjeev introduced me to all of them. I wasn't either a client or an organizer!

I had never been a part of professional hiking group before, till now. All we did was to pack our backpack and start hauling it on our ars, up the valley. There were no briefings, no do's and don'ts, no time limits and of course no 'sweeper', the term I heard for the first time when Naresh told them that he will take the position of sweeper! Initially I thought it was more related to the cooking department, but later I understood its actual meaning in hiking parlance. A sweeper is a person who is solely responsible to bring the last person of a hiking group safely along.

As the crew was busy in loading the draft animals, mules and Spiti horses, I could hear them whispering, what the hell was inside these rucksack? Someone guessed bottle of liquor and someone joked, huge stones, for the weight was simply unbearable. Poor animals, luckily doesn't have brains for wild guesses.

Most of the trekkers were carrying professional cameras, and won't let any moment go without a click.

One of the guys was a Vet like me. Aha! Two Vets. Aren't we adventure lovers? I thought.

The group was homogeneous in terms of their likings but not so, fitness wise. The youngest trekker might have weighed more than a quarter past quintals.

After having a small lunch the hike stated. Reticence, as always, was my hallmark. I was more concentrated about my chances of conquering the Pass. I followed Sanjeev as we moved up through thickets of fir jungle. But the pace of trekkers receded with passing time. They would stop anywhere, and took photographs till that perfect picture. Was it a resting technique or profound love for photography I wondered? Most of the trekkers were exhausted soon and a few cut off the weight of their rucksack. Perhaps altitude was taking its toll and why not, after all Mount Kinabalu, the highest peak of Malaysia measure only 4000 odd meters above sea level.

To me terrain looked like Bhaba valley, Kinnaur, flora almost similar.

We finally reached camp one named *Chhika* around six PM. A beautiful knoll besides little stream, a high peak scrapping the sky in the backdrop called *Indra Quila* (The bastion of Lord Indra). Tents for the clients were already pitched and exquisite aroma of myriad dishes was fuming from the kitchen tent. Hot tea was served immediately. Staff was busy in preparing fresh snacks, well garnished and presented as if the clients were resting in some ensconced liar.

After sipping tea I erected my tent next to the kitchen. Thankfully my younger brother brought this *two men* tent a few months ago.

Sanjeev asked me if I mind to sleep with staff inside kitchen, for the clients might need an extra tent as the organizers has forgotten to carry spare one. I nodded instantly, for I was also a part of the organizers, though unofficially. The clients were treated with utmost care, be it in terms of meals, logistics, hot water etc. A makeshift toilet tent was also established. I helped the kitchen guys with preparing meals.

Guests were served around 8.30 PM, only after that, we had our fill. It was really great to be in nature's lap again, but here at camp one, almost 50 tents were pitched, many of them permanently, by big adventure companies. A *dhaba* was also available just above my tent. Fortunately the clients got adjusted in their tents and mine was spared. Soon after dinner I occupied my tent and retired for the day. It was 10.30 PM.

It was a clear beautiful sunny morning next day. We were to hike up to camp two, just beneath *Hamta* Pass. Clients were already out of their tents by 6.40 am, to capture the serene and blissful morning view in their cameras but to me it was only the lens of my eyes and the memories of my mind.

We started the hike at 8.45 am. Though distance was around five to six kilometres but the elevation was steeper. Clients kept progressing slowly up the hill putting their equipments to maximum use. Their rucksack, which was no less than a mystery to the staffers, actually carried these heavy photography equipments. Actually the clients were part of a professional photography group back at Malaysia.

In the afternoon weather started to brew up. Grey clouds shrouded the sky and a mild drizzle started immediately which turned into heavy rain in no time. My light weighted *quechua* poncho played its role and all the hikers were covered in myriad colors of their raincoats. Wafting fog was ethereal, displaying a constant affair with barren rocks high up on the mountains.

Today, hiking party was strong except hefty guy, Farhan. One or the other guide would always encourage him mid way. I was of the opinion that if someone was going to turn back, it would be him.

We had to cross a glacial rivulet on the way to camp two, amid incessant rain. Though I was well versed with mountain streams but yet it was much fierce owing to heavy downpour up hills. And to Malaysian clients it must have been horrific. We found one old man with pulley and rope at the bank of river. A hundred rupees he would charge to slide past torrent, not a bad deal for the foreigners, given the magnitude of gushing water. However Sanjeev would not stay behind to drew the adrenaline through his veins as he led the small daring party consisting of all locals and a few clients, chained hand to hand, braving the gorge with anchoring each foot as much stronger as possible over boulder strewn river bed. I felt the sheer force of roaring stream, much avid to take us along. It was indeed thrilling. But at the same time, I learnt how to cross a river with human chain formation, facing the upstream.

Equally thrilling was crossing it with a rope. Clients enjoyed the small glide with numerous *selfies*.

Once we crossed the river, packed lunch was served to the clients; vegetable, fruits and boiled eggs. I munched my favorite roasted grams with *elaichi dana* stashed in the deep pocket of my bag.

Hereafter trek was gentle. Most of the clients excelled comfortably as the sky cleared, but Mr. Farhan was ambling assiduously with his face turned completely red. Initially I tried to give him a company, kept him occupied with my queer arguments, but then it needed much patience to continue with his snail's pace. Subsequently he was left to the duty bound, head guide Sanjeev.

We reached camp two, *Balu Ka ghera* (literally; the siege of bears, though we didn't saw any), a small basin beneath the *Hamta* Pass around 4.00 PM. Camp was already set, hot tea served immediately and of course well garnished snacks only to the clients. I pitched my tent in line with the clients and took some time off to the basin, where many small and large tents were erected, a few permanent ones. A small *dhaba* embellished the area towards the east, not so frequent at such altitude. I saw one small tent, on a hillock, bit higher to the basin, and walked towards it inquisitively. A bearded, affable young man sat outside; trying to get some warmth from his cooking burner's flame. I had seen him at camp one earlier. He was a solo trekker from Mumbai.

Ribin was a former Jet Airways employee with handsome salary, before the airways were gutted and employees struck off the roll. To him it was a blessing in disguise, for he had always loved to venture in the wild, all alone. He told me many stories of his solo adventures across different states of India. He had explored the Himalayas in different parts of Northern India including Uttrakhand, Himachal and Ladakh region; most of it solo. In my life I had never known any solo trekker till now. He was content and complacent, without any regret for the lacking luxuries of metropolitan life. He never planned anything like all of us. When I asked him where he will move next, he told, may be towards *Spiti* valley or maybe he will stay here itself, for next one or two days if he feels so. He showed me all the survival equipments that he owned, be it small solar battery charger, *Go pro*, small burner with butane canisters and of course half a dozen books! He was preparing *Chana dal* (black gram) at such heights oblivious about fuel shortage or the heavy loads of ration he was carrying all the way. He would need one porter for crossing the pass, he admitted. With the usual promise of meeting again, I turned towards my tent. Twilight had already set.

Soon the clients were served hot meals, well wrapped in aluminum foil, inside big splendid mess tent, while we waited till they all were finished. We cuddled in small kitchen tent and savored the meals while young staffers exchanging banters in between. Sky was overcast as I slipped inside my sleeping bag, excited about big Pass day tomorrow.

Next morning I got up to buzzing shrill of some kind. What was happening outside, I wondered. As I unzipped my small tent, I saw a few clients standing near mess tent;

watching intently towards the sky. Someone amongst them was flying a drone. Those days, drone was a rarity. I got out of my tent and appreciated this beautiful morning. It must have been a charismatic top view from the eyes of drone.

We started the hike at 8.15 am sharp, I and Sanjeev leaving the camp at the end. We caught the party soon. I trailed for long till that big glacier on which a flock of sheep was passing majestically on its way back to lower plains. And then I took long strides to reach the front with team leader Naresh Sharma. Clients were excelling satisfactorily except big guy Farhan. I along with other young boy, a local trained mountaineer was assigned the task of bringing him along.

Soon it started to drizzle and we wrapped our backpacks with rain covers. As per head guide, it would take a couple of hours to reach the top, which I considered four, given the pace of our party. The massive peaks above the pass were snow capped and colossal to the extent that they all were shrouded with mist and clouds. One of the peaks named *Indra Asana* is six thousand odd meters.

After negotiating the final steep glacier strenuously, party finally reached the Pass where Sanjeev was waiting exuberantly.

After half an hour I was on the crest of the Pass. I stood among haphazard stone cairns above a serac edge and looked far down into black and white Lahaul valley. An ethereal view it was indeed. Farhan was also inching towards the top with local young chap, against all my perceptions.

I saluted to his perseverance and steel *will.*

Videos, *selfies* were taken while the foreigners unfurled their national flag and so did we. What a moment it was, at least to the clients who must have scaled the highest ever peak in their life. I posed my all time favourite, *sheersh asana* (the head stand) on a narrow ledge besides Pass, in supplication to the God of Mountains. The barren Lahaul valley was visible to the other side.

Descend was pretty easier. After a little criss-crossing amid scree and boulders, we encountered a small glacier, which we skid off gaily, as we reached the basin of this valley. Naresh guide's techniques of handling the ice proved beneficial.

Hereafter it was a straight walk towards the camping site along glacial river.

On the way, I talked to one of my Kuala Lumpur friend, Mr. Rafael Rahman about his profession, personal and social life, how they planned the journey and of course expenses involved. This is what one gets in a professional tour. Comradery. We reached the camping site at 6.15 pm, peaks still sparkling with evening sun.

Cold wind was blowing fiercely as I pitched my tent facing river and the magnificent brownish peaks past it. Too much of permanent tents were pitched around hence no more solace. Soon I found the *Solo* man Ribin pitching his tent on a beautifully perched location. He hired a porter and a mule at camp two, this morning.

It was our last camping night. Organizers were happy that whole party made it to the Pass and reached here uneventfully, what better can be expected. Perhaps they were happy with me as well, for I served them to some extent one way or another. After dinner, I wrote my diary in dim mobile light and before resting, lied down under star lit night for a brief moment as I could watch the galaxies too close to me. My mum must be watching from somewhere above.

Early morning view of camp three, named *Shiya ghorey,* literally means cold home, was incredible. As I unzipped the door top of my tent, I watched serene river, flowing gracefullywith sound of incessant clatters cutting across the valley. High peaks with needle sharp cornices adorned the margins of this world. A little bird perched just in front of my tent in search of early morning feast. Gradually the valley glittered with the golden sun rays. Water of the flowing river sparkled like metal with each ripple. Weather was quite clear and the cold winds had ceased. I wondered how beautiful life almighty had bestowed upon us. As I scribbled my daily notes relaxing inside my tent, watching big old glacier in the backdrop, the amateur shutterbugs from Malaysia were out on the bank of river with their heavy photography equipments to capture every moment of this incredible morning. In fact at night they were busy in taking photographs of stars, constellations, galaxy and all other celestial bodies visible. I saw a few snaps, which were quite amazing. I also tried to take some photographs of night sky with my cell Phone, but result was as expected, a black screen.

After enjoying *Maggi*, egg *bhurji* and *pulao* at breakfast we proceeded towards *Chhatru*, the end point of this trek, where this rivulet would meet with *Chandra* river, flowing from Lahaul region. Soon we had to cross the stream, which was not that much deep but the water was freezing cold. As I was the last person in the orthodox human chain formed to cross the river, I could not move as quickly as desired, henceforth it turned my feet completely numb.

Hereafter the descent was quite gentle. I was still quite unsure which way to go after *Chhatru*, as one way would lead to *Spiti*, Kaza, and other back to Manali. The horse man cautioned me to reach *Chhatru* by 11.00 am so that I could catch the bus up to Kaza. He told that the total distance between *Chhatru* and Kaza was around 250 odd kilometers, and only one bus ply between Manali and Kaza. Considering the facts it was obvious that the bus would be thronged up to Kaza. Given the thin chances of a comfortable journey, I reached to the conclusion of getting back to Manali with entire team.

After moderate walk of an hour from camp three, we saw the highway across *Chandra* river. We appreciated many tents pitched at *Chhatru,* for this place served the base camp for coveted*Chandra Tal* lake in *spiti* valley.

We reached at *Chhatru* around half past noon. A cab and a gypsy were waiting for us. Whole the team was happy on this small victory. We admired each other, exchanged contacts, and wished to meet again. What a beautiful journey it had been.

We boarded the transport and reached back to Manali *via* blissful *Rohtang* Pass. A huge traffic jam was encountered at *Marhi*, thanks to the inundate tourists and the road repair work. Mobile signal popped up only after *Marhi*, thus landing us back to social life after three days.

I talked briefly to my family back home and left a message to friend at Manali, for my uncharged battery exhausted sooner. Finally I was dropped at my friend's motel in Manali, by half past five. A strange sense of detachment prevailed.

It was a memorable journey indeed. I had three nightout in the wild, made many friends not only locally but globally as well. Until four days ago, I never knew who Mr. Sanjeev or Mr. Naresh were? Or where the place *Hamta* lies, or who Mr. Ribin the *soloer* was or what Mr. Rafael, the man from Kuala Lumpur does? Never did I watched before, the sheer determination that Mr. Farhan exhibited in this tour. I happily survived with two square meals a day without any complaint.

I introspected, did self-appraisal throughout this journey and also evaluated my physical fitness.

Though it was a professional trekking tour, I lived with a sense of perfect freedom and deep physical and mental well-being.

I wanted nothing except equanimity.

Remote Habitation: Rupin Pass

Once, when I was on my solo hiking trip to *Bhaba-Pin* pass, I met one affable, stout bodied, lanky fellow guiding a small party through the same pass near *Mudh* village in Pin valley. We didn't talk much except the mandatory intro and exchange of pleasantries. After 2-3 days when I was waiting for my early morning bus towards Shimla, at bus station Kaza, I identified the same figure hovering around. Inquisitively, I asked where he was heading for. He told me that he was from Rohru, Dodra-Kawar region, the remotest area of district Shimla, HP; and was working as professional trekking guide. As he had successfully led the clients across high *Bhaba-Pin* pass, he was now returning back to his village.

The only bus towards Shimla from Kaza started at 7.00 am and reached Rekongpeo around 5.00 pm. I got down at *Powari*, a small station at NH-05 below Rekongpeo, for I was in a hurry to catch another early bus towards Shimla. Again that fellow was standing beside me, for he was also getting late. He had to halt at Rampur tonight, for the last bus towards Rohru had already left and he had to catch the first bus early next morning. From Rampur to Rohru, it's a complete circumnavigation through thick forest and rugged terrain. Road conditions were not good and the travel was not comfortable. Instead, he thought about reaching up to Sangla village in Baspa valley, Kinnaur and then to cross Rupin Pass; for it was the shortest route to his village and the beautiful trail was of course the hikers delight. A bus to Sangla was about to reach here and he was firm now to board it, instead of heading towards Rampur Bushahar. At one though I was very much excited to join him and cross the pass, but then I was away from home for considerably large span and astraying further would have conjured hue and cry back home. But I was fascinated by the way he described the Rupin Pass.

Lately, I was being asked by a few hiking freaks to guide them through *Bhaba-Pin* pass, but I was reluctant to tread the same as I had been to this trail at least three-four times now. However, as the fall was at threshold and the hiking season was about to finish, a small expedition was expected, and which other moment could have been best than to explore much coveted Rupin Pass.

I contacted the old hiking partners and revealed my plans on a short notice. Vijesh Guruji agreed instantaneous, though Kulwinder Negi took some time. We hired a guide from Sangla, who would lead us up to the Rupin top and show the trail ahead. Though I was comfortable with exploring the area at our own, but the boys thought otherwise. They wanted to be sure for the recent news of trekkers being rescued in this terrain was replete. We had already explored the other side of Baspa valley while we circumambulated the *Kinnaur Kailash* through *Charang La*, many years ago.

Second weekend of September 2022 was chosen to start the assault.

We boarded the first bus to Sangla from Rampur Bushahar and reached there around 11.30 am. A 4x4 camper vehicle was hired up to *Sangla Kanda*, the last motorable point; a sizable distance of six to seven kilometers was reduced henceforth. The guide was supposed to meet us at Sangla. This all was thankfully co-ordinated by one of my staffer Mr Bihari Lal, stationed there.

After having a spicy lunch at local *dhaba,* we purchased needed fresh vegetables and other essential food items. The hired vehicle which was supposed to take us around noon came after an hour's delay. Finally our journey towards *Sangla Kanda* started at 1.00 pm. The local guide with whom I had a conversation this morning told me that he won't be accompanying us due to personal exigencies but would send his cousin instead.

Raj was a young reticent local boy who brought another kid, Ankit with him, so that he gets company in his return journey as we had hired him only up to Rupin pass thus they ought to turn back hereafter.

The view of Sangla valley was mesmerizing from the other side of Baspa river as we moved through thick forest of deodar and rhododendron. *Sangla Kanda* is summer paradise both panorama and weather wise. Cool breeze was blowing as we bumped inside an old Bolero Camper on *kutcha* road. Around 3.15 pm we started the final hike. Our guide told us that it would take one hour to reach first camping site, but to save summit day's time we had to ascend one hour more to reach next camping site.

I was not to the best of my physical fitness, for I could feel the sprain in my knees, thanks to rough regular football session back at my place. Also my left shoulder was pinching intermittently. In fact just before this tour I was skeptical about any final expedition of this season due to health issues. Also I was carrying the loads of camping material and cooking equipments, for Guruji was already quibbling for his sedentary lifestyle and Kulwinder hadn't hiked a hill for last many years. So they put entire onus of hauling the load upon me.

Trail from *Sangla Kanda* to camp 1 was gentle and grade moderate. We reached this place around 4.30 pm, but kept excelling towards high camp. I could feel my heart thudding vigorously as the air was getting thinner above tree line. At one point where a mild stream was trickling down, we decided to set the camp as the next camping site was not visible and the dusk was about to set. We erected the tents quickly and it was time to prepare dinner. Guide and his assistant would sleep in their own tent, but the meals were to be prepared for all. My kerosene stove was chugging well but ought to be pumped intermittently to maintain the pressure. As the dusk sat, we appreciated ochre sky towards the west. Dark big mountains were shrouding the pass towards east. Temperature started to fall gradually with the night. However the local distillate that we carried along from Sangla proved beneficial. We enjoyed the dinner in milky lunar light. Around 10 pm we moved towards our respective tents and retired for the day immediately as the scheduled time for summit day was fixed at six in the morning.

It was a sound sleep indeed. I got up around 5.00 am. It was pitch dark outside but the weather was perfect. Those icy winds that blew late night had ceased. Vijesh Guruji mustered the courage to prepare early morning tea as we still kept resting inside our tents. We had a light breakfast of bread and tea, and finally broke the camp at 6.15 am. Assistant guide volunteered to carry our tent giving much respite to my aching shoulder.

As we meandered through the beautiful glades of Sangla Kanda the first ray of light hit upon us. We captured the sunrise view in our cameras and started to ascend above a small stream called *Rontigaad*. Once we scaled a small knoll, we saw the Rupin Pass sprawling majestically towards the west, embellished with many cairns and prayer flags. Towards the north another high pass, the *Gunas Pass*, with treacherous terrain lied. It would lead to *Janglik* village in Chirgaon sub-division traversing the *Chanshal* pass. En-route one would find seven beautiful *Chander Nahan* lakes. We tried to scale*Gunas* pass route many years ago from Janglik side, but couldn't finish it off. May be some other day, I thought.

Like other passes, here were no glaciers this time. We negotiated scree zone before reaching the pass. We all regretted to watch naked peaks and valleys around. How damn blissful the view would have been, had the glaciers been here. The only exalting thing was to watch numerous *Bramha Kamals* blooming; just beneath the pass, spared by the ruminants. At 9.15 am we reached the pass. We rested for a while, took some photographs and as the fog started to swirl through the natural 'funnel' shaped terrain towards the other side of the pass, we bade farewell to our guide and his assistant, only after paying exorbitantly for their services. The height of Rupin pass is around 4800 meters, equivalent to the highest elevation I had camped last year. I didn't appreciate any headache this time.

Descend through the 'funnel' was quite comfortable, for the trail was wide and scree free. We marked two big boulders down the valley across a small stream where we would rest and take some refreshments. Within an hour we had crossed the last moraine and now could see a beautiful lush green bugyal, *Dhanderas Thach* below. But then to reach there, we had to descend perilous trail across huge waterfall. Descend was not comfortable as I started to limp painfully under heavy load as I was carrying the tent again. Moreover the pressure on left knee and left shoulder was now unbearable. As we moved down past a shepherd's *dera*, we saw a mesmerizing waterfall flowing gallantly with deafening sound down to the valley. The view was so infatuating that we watched it unmoved at least for an hour. It is perhaps the best view of this whole trek.

After crossing the waterfall through switchback trail, we finally descended to vast expanse of the plain valley. It was the lush green pasture of *Dhanderas Thach* pervading across now gently flowing Rupin river. We were extremely tired due to constant steep descent, thus halted briefly to take some rest. View of the waterfall from this place was just awesome. I threw my heavy load aside and ran towards the stream, to immerse my aching feet in glacial water with the hope to get some relief. It was really soothing. We prepared a *Maggi* lunch under a boulder beside the stream. Two local shepherds joined us and reassured that we could easily make it up to *Jakha* today or even down to last motor able point, *Jiskun*. We were resolute and motivated.

At around 2pm we finally got up and started the journey ahead. Hereafter it was all about walking beside Rupin river. The grade was gentle and the terrain was comfortable. I kept leading briskly almost for an hour, as the partners were reluctant to move ahead. Suddenly I felt a bit bloated, and the sheer pain in the knee and shoulder propped up. I felt like I should stop then and there. I threw my rucksack apart and prostrated on a big boulder. I could hear my heart thudding loudly. What had happened? There was no headache. Partners were yet to arrive and all I wanted to have was a thorough rest. I wished we would have camped here.

Soon the partners came and shared my concern. But all they wanted was to get down to *Jhaka* village as soon as possible. We were told that the only ascent we would encounter before the village was after crossing a bridge over this stream. So we kept excelling, with the hope that the bridge would come soon. Balsam grass was growing tall every now and then; depicting it would have been resting place for the flocks of sheep and goat earlier.

After walking for almost a couple of hours, we still couldn't reach the small bridge. My aches were a bit mellowed now and I could feel the vigor again. My strides were brisk and sure. We reached thick forested area where government had built some huts though not looked after very well but good resting place for shepherd and the nomads indeed. This place is called as *Burans Kandi*, and rightly so as we found many dwarf rhododendrons growing around. Landscape was just awesome, but we were not having enough time to appreciate the vista. And now I was literally gliding down the valley with the hope that the bridge would come soon. It was almost a jog. Soon Vijesh caught me and while matching my pace yelled that we have to move fast.

"What?" I screamed involuntarily. "What could be faster than this? Do you want us to jog all the way down to *Jakha*? What's the hurry for, man? What is the fun of trekking when you are not appreciating the aura around? For past three-four hours all we are concentrating about is our trail. What is the point of reaching back home tomorrow itself? Had some adverse conditions prevailed above, had we been able to reach up to this point?" I threw flurry of questions over him in sheer frustration, still walking quickly. He was taken by surprise. I was actually not content with the way this expedition has initiated. It was not at all an expedition for we had taken the help of guides; hence no excitements of finding a trail. Secondly, they couldn't spare extra time to wander in the wild, for the home affairs were priority. These both logics were well against my thoughts of being in wilderness. Time should never be a barrier. Carry enough food to survive a few extra days and camp wherever you feel relaxed. And here, we were running.

After half an hour of quick jog (Kulwinder was actually running) we saw the small bridge. This place is called as *Udaknal.* We sat past bridge to catch some breathe. Exhaustion couldn't be denied any more. We discussed the prospect of reaching the village and decided to camp wherever we could find appropriate place. Now it was a steep ascent through deodar forest. It was 5 pm and the sun was gradually advancing towards the horizon. We couldn't find any place to pitch the tent even after an hour. Now the trail was wide and straight. We were told that it would take 45 minutes to reach the village from bridge; I considered it one and half an hour, which means we were near to the village now. Soon we saw d*ogri*'s of the villagers, fields growing with local crops of *Fafra, Koda*, and *Chulai*. All strength came back again.

We met two youngsters just ahead of the village. As they saw us they offered us apples that they were relishing. Jitender *alias* Johnty, work as temporary guide cum kitchen staff with seasonal trekking company. He explained to us about how the trekking routs are operated in this area either from Dehradun, Uttarakhand side or recently from Rohru, Himachal side. We were standing almost at the border of Himachal, as the next mountain beyond Rupin river belong to Uttrakhand state. It was really surprising to know that here people feel more attached and comfortable to move to Dehradun than to Shimla, for the barrier *Chanshal Pass* poses the great threat, more so during long winters. We were told that this remote area of Dodra-Kawar was a part of Garhwal *riyasat* long back before the king bestowed it upon the princess who was married to the prince of Rampur *riyasat.*

Here we found the flickering mobile signal of BSNL. Johnty accompanied us towards a small playground above the village which was replete with young chaps playing volleyball and other games. Dusk was about to set. No one was startled or inquisitive to see us; rather we were surprised why no one was giving a damn. Later we found that trekking and camping is a routine activity in this part of the world since long, hence people are very much used to such affairs. Had the trail been not commercialized here, perhaps it would have been the real tribal region given the tough terrain and remote topography.

Johnty assisted us in setting the camp. It was dark by now. We were tired to extreme and all we wanted were to slip inside our sleeping bags. As soon as our *Dal* was ready the kerosene stove gave way. We tried to pump it incessantly but to no success. Finally we had to be content with savoring *Dal* and bread. Last drops of local potion were helpful in alleviating the exhaustion to some extent. Another surprising thing that we found here was, not many people enjoyed liquor, smoke or non vegetarian diet. The influence of a sect was so much prevailing that old traditional tribal culture, though barbaric it might have been, was abjured. So in my view livestock rearing was totally a commercial activity here, for people won't eat it themselves. At around 10pm we retired for the day. As per Johnty's calculation we must have walked around thirty five kilometers today.

We got up around 5 o'clock in the morning and without breakfasting; owing to kerosene stove malfunction, broke the camp. The descent down to *Jiskun* village, the motor able point, was quite blissful even when the muscles were aching. We ought to reach *Jiskun* by 8 am as the only vehicle plying towards Rohru would leave by this time. We had contacted the driver last evening with the help of Johnty.

Jiskun is a small pristine village situated amidst thick fir and deodar jungle. Many ridges past Rupin river; belonging to Uttrakhand were visible towards the west. The last village of Himachal, *Pandhaar*, lies hidden beyond treacherous peak. We wondered whether it would ever get connected with the road.

Finally at 8.00 am Prithviraj, the cherubic driver sporting pony tail hair style beneath colorful bandana, appeared behind the wheel of his *Force Trax* named 'Rupin Adventure'. We loaded our luggage over the roof and huddled inside, for other passengers also started to throng. Here everyone knew everyone. People are physically fit and leaner. We failed to remember any face with pot belly. Even young school children walk from *Jakha* to *Jiskun* every day, for the only government secondary school is situated here. The 'Rupin Adventure' started well past the scheduled time and further earnest its name when we were told to get down mid way as Prithvi had to turn back to bring an ailing lady. Medical exigencies here are the real ones. The main hospital lies sixty to seventy kilometres away at Rohru that also after crossing high *Chanshal* pass. We felt the pain and fear that people apprehend here during long winters. They ought to take the detour via Uttrakhand along Rupin river.

We reached Rohru at 3.00 pm. Last bus to our destination, Rampur Bushahar, had already left at two o'clock. So it was time for well deserved celebration after successful expedition, at Rohru itself. We headed towards some shacks erected along the bank of river *Pabbar*. A swimming pool lured us with lukewarm water. All we needed to get relaxed was to have a thorough bath, and where else would have we got such an opportunity?

Winter Blues

With the end of *Hamta* Pass expedition my summer sojourn for the year 2019 was almost over, for it was the month of September and the fall was at threshold. A long winter was expected. My diary entry for 27.11.2019, 9:28 am

"Greyish brown clouds all over the sky. White sheet up to Thaach Village, overlooking my balcony. Chhonda (a little hamlet above Nigulsari) also painted white, what an incredible view! Temperature has plummeted considerably. Could feel the numbness in my fingers while using toilet water. First snowfall of the winter 2019-2020, a long journey ahead."

I kept myself busy with mom's convalescence. She was undergoing treatment for her ailment at Indira Gandhi Medical College and HospitalShimla for past one year. With passing October mom's condition only deteriorated. She was diagnosed with bilateral ovarian cancer in the year 2018 and was being administered chemotherapy routinely at IGMC Shimla.

Infact response to the initial treatment was highly appreciable. She recovered to the extent that within six months she thought about rearing cattle, poultry and other livestock; post retirement and also growing some more saplings in our orchard. But then this dreaded disease does not parry away so easily. After PET scan at Chandigarh, the lesion left were found quite miniscule but significant. Even a speck of cancerous cell can pose utmost threat of proliferation which is difficult to contain second time. Initially we kept waiting and observed the nature of these *left overs*, but as subsequent tests showed it was surging again. So, some other chemotherapeutic drugs were introduced after recommended cycles.

CA 125 level (marker for cancerous cell invasion) kept increasing. She won't find that comfort at home and those intermittent abdominal burning sensation would persist. By the month of December, she was hospitalized at least couple of times. These chemotherapeutic drugs kills all growing cells including RBC'sand there often used to be sheer shortage of blood even at Blood bank Shimla, her beingA B negative group. With my liaisons and contacts I arranged many units whenever needed but then the requirement was well beyond availability. I ran from pillar to post, literally, in order to arrange the same, for its not a commodity that one can buy with money, exorbitant what may be, but a thing that only develops in human body. My diary note 23.01.2020,

"*From 'first breath' hospital to 'last breath' hospital. It's not strange when you have to traverse all the way to collect fresh blood, between inceptions of life to cessation of life. Kamla Nehru Hospital (KNH, Shimla), the only Govt. Gyanaecology and obstetrics department, is the hospital where people come to celebrate beginning of a new life, a new entrant to this world. Whereas at Oncology, IGMC, it's all about palliative care, all efforts to enhance life; how so ever painful, qualitatively miserable it may be. So, presently at KNH for one more unit of blood. Two units already donated by two benevolent super human, Mr Manjot Singh and Dr Robin. Still many units needed in coming days..*"

I myself was ready to donate blood but they won't take it even for replacement. So common, B positive! Then I came to know about Blood donors group and contacted them. They helped magnanimously and are still helping selflessly the needy patients. They really feel exasperated, if they could not arrange any! I became a member of this group and had donated many times since then.

Diary entry on New year eve, 31.12.2019, Chemotherapy ward IGMC,

"*...all sorts of patients here, irrespective of gender, age, ethnicity, religion, cast, economy and topography. What traditional what modern, all are lying here, waiting for their turns, to be cannulated and injected with drugs. At times it seems that this unit is a kind of recharge center like we find for our gadgets, one come exhausted, hopeless and move recharged, full of hopes.........Boys have planned to celebrate the last day (of the year) back at District headquarters RekongPeo, I was really enthusiastic but really more than happy to watch new hopes dawning upon Mum in this new year...It's party time indeed. 31st December 2019. Myself and mom. A bowl full of rajmah, butter, curd, khichdi and chapatis. We relished it only after taking the mandatory selfies. I am really enjoying it, no more scruples and qualms. What better could be than to stay back with ailing mom! Happiness is not always cheering up with friends while raising toast, it's* *about being with the person that really matters, most reverend your parents."*

Winter was harsh that year. Snowfall was immense to the extent that capital smart city was frozen up to four days. Not even emergency vehicles were able to ply on slippery frozen roads. At one point of time myself, Ranjana and Mom were struck at *Boileauganj*, our departmental guest house just five kilometres away from IGMC for more than 24 hours in deep snow outside, with mum's unbearable pain and cries all night. How helpless we felt against the fury of nature. Even emergency services, 108, spell helplessness. I would come out and move carefully in knee deep snow up to National Highway junction and watch if it was opened for traffic; every couple of hours, but the situation remained grim. Only in the evening an ambulance from NGO *Almighty blessings* responded and with the help of my good friend Devinder, we took mom to the hospital ultimately.

Thereafter my place for night rest was not-so-nicely-mopped oncology floor where no one ever dreamt to be. In the day I would run for arranging the blood or routine errands for diagnostic tests, only to lie down over the floor along with other attendants at night, exhaustively tired. Sometimes we woke up only to watch a white snow sheet outside. Thank god the ward was thermostat and no feel of any cold was observed inside. The only worry was rat and cockroach infestations, usual thing in Govt. institutions.

With the advent of New Year 2020, Mom's condition deteriorated exponentially. Her both feet turned oedematous (swell), and now she suffered constant vomiting. Even if she swallowed a sip of water, it was bound to come out. But she still seems content and her sheer zeal to fight it out was as ever. She survived all the life threatening situations in her early life, that one may think about; be it a Snake bite, Scorpio bite, Scrub typhus or extreme burns, and faced all with brave heart. A born fighter, never give up kind of lady she was. I took leaves from my office and was stationed at IGMC with mum permanently.

Now the snarled corridor, the filthy bath and loo, the not-so-clean floor of oncology has become familiar and that sense of abhorrence had gone. I never felt awkward being there. Even staff now recognized me. I used to follow up the cases of adjacent patients and would pronounce the ray of hope. At times, I would act queerly and ask all sorts of questions from nursing students and explain to them what medical knowledge I had with me, thoroughly. Gradually those small kids would keep looking for me, strange bond human beings can find, even in extreme conditions. I found no trauma or stigma while lying down on the floor of cancer ward at night; in fact I used to motivate newcomers as well. I had become a veteran of this ward given the time period I spent there. Even staff loved me, be it Bhupi bhai the sweeper, Sister Nisha, Mr. Chitranja; the technician, Dr Era, Dr Damini, Dr Naina, Dr Vivek; the residents or Dr Dhiman; the consultant.

The pharmacy man Mr. Abhishek and Mr. Harish became good friends; salutes were exchanged involuntary whenever we met. It was a tacit sense of selfless camaraderie that developed gradually over time. I was really enjoying my stay there, for mum was in front of my eyes and I could assist her in all possible ways, be it about taking her to the washroom, washing her face, massaging her back, and feeding her frequently even when the vomiting episodes continued. She also felt comfortable with me as ever. My contentment with the surroundings may be attributed to my hiking expeditions. You are rarely concerned about any luxury around and it's only about enjoying the survival, moment by moment. That's what these expeditions teach you. More content, more rugged you are, less exasperated you become in any given situation.

But mental trauma with regard to constant fall in mother's condition prevailed. Somewhere deep in the core of my heart I dithered with the future prospect, but it was Mum who would react as if she was not going to give up so easily. That provided the needed impetus and we both enjoyed every moment.

By February she has grown really weak. Her gaunt body would scare many, but the steel will persisted. We bantered, we joked, we giggled, we cajoled but never wept, for we cherished each-others company. Perhaps I was fortunate enough to help her in the time when she needed it most. I spent a thorough quality time with mum in this one and a half year period than rest of my life.

That winter I wished Mom to recover by next summer and I would explore the Himalayas carefree in more intense manner, along with self exploration.

But destiny had written something else, though.

Mom left us all to her heavenly abode on 29th of March 2020; along with her all the wishes to go for high altitude pilgrimage, for she would always ask me to take her along someday, were put to rest. In Buddhist *Nygma* school's teaching. The *Bardo Thodol*, the Tibetan book of death, the transition from this life to next life is described in exhaustive detail. Those who understands and apply the teachings, 'death' unfolds not as a tragic end but as a transition from this life to the next. By approach the body's end with a calm and informed mind, by seeing it for what it is, a manifestation of impermanence, death become something not to fear but to resolutely accept. Death is a lesson.

Even her ashes couldn't be immersed in the holy Ganges at *Haridwar*, for it was nationwide curfew and lock down due to eruption of a dreaded pandemic COVID-19.

The unfathomable void could never be filled, but that sense of relinquishment can only be sought in high Himalayas, for now I know, running from something never bring comprehension. Consciously practicing in the intimacy of what you want to understand is the surest part to wisdom.

Jono Lineen has rightly said that, '*Simple faith is empowering; but one dimensional, while the considered faith, one derives from self exploration, is a belief you can call your own, something that will survive the storm of everyday life.*'

Himalayan Biodiversity: Challenges & Resolution

The blissfulness of living in the Himalaya has been described by many authors vivaciously since time immemorial, be it in terms of seeking solitude, self-realization, and peace of mind or ultimate *Nirvana*. Since ancient times, people had walked all across geo-political map, to be within the lap of Himalayan ranges. For the denizens, mountains are the true meaning of life, in fact the life – naurisher itself. Our ancestors dwell and survived through the hardship of mountain life and learnt the ways and means of living with it in consonance. In comparison to fertile plainer region down the river basin, barren rocky terrain makes it difficult to inhabit in such area.

The diverse climate and varied environmental conditions of the Himalaya support diverse habitat and ecosystem with equally diverse life forms. It provides an important habitat to flora and fauna including 9000 species of angiosperms and hence, is considered as the hot –spot of biodiversity. There are about 3470 species considered exclusively endemic to the Himalaya.

People adopted animal husbandry practices at large, for the land holdings for agriculture was much less and the crops grown are exclusively adapted to that particular altitude. The Breed characteristics developed as per the natural selection, to thrive in these difficult areas.

Rampur bushair, Gaddi, Chang-thangi and Chegu are few registered local sheep breeds and Charmurti horses/ Spiti horsesis one of the breed of equine, which is well adapted to survive in harsh conditions of cold desert. People in Kinnaur and Spiti valley rely much over these draught animals, for these being hardy and sure footed are the only means of transportation and carriage to remote areas. The breeding tract of these Ponies is mainly in Pin valley, Spiti. For conservation of this indigenous breed, Department of Animal Husbandry is running a Farm at Lari, Spiti.

Local barley, millets, *Koda* (Eleusinecorocana), *Ogla* (Buckwheat), *Fapra* (Fogopyrumesculentum), *Bathu* (Chenopodiumalbum) and *Tulsi* (Osimumsanctum) still constitute the staple diet, particularly in remote and tribal Himalayan region.

High Alpine pasture of the Himalaya provides much needed nutritious forages to livestock in brief summer, for only in this period high valleys are accessible for grazing purpose. The pasture land of these valleys has been explored by local shepherds' long time ago, as these are the only life line to their livestock, in terms of much needed nutritious diet after long snowbound winter spell, when all the reserves has been exhausted, and it's high time to invigorate the body before the fall, as the coming winters; who know is much harsher.

Shepherds must have been the earliest explorers. The inquisitiveness of knowing the unknown, led them to new valleys, for the challenge also brought opportunity to reach new fertile lands never grazed before.

Himalayan highland is also a heaven for wild herbal plants and yet-to-be-explored flora. Historically, usage of Himalayan medicinal plants dates very long back. Written records of Himalayan plants being used as medicine are found in *Rigveda* texts around 6,500 years ago. Ethno-medicinal usage of various herbs, percolate down through many generations till date. In my numerous jaunts to various passes and valleys of Kinnaur district, I was blessed enough to get some knowledge about these herbs used for treating various ailments by local folks. Lately when more emphasis was given to Ayurveda and Homeopathy, the value of these herbs only increased. The illegal collection and sale of these medicinal plants still continue, surreptitiously. Earlier it was *Nag Chhatri* (Trilliumgovanianum), but recently it's *Kadvi,* which is in much demand in local marketsthese days. We saw many localites camping high in the snow capped valleys, ransacking these herbs for months together. Nobody knew where exactly it is finally shipped and what it is used for. *Chukhri* roots are pestled into ointment and it act as anti-inflammatory. Tuberous roots of *Jaddi dhup* (Jurineamacrocephala) is used as incense. *Jungli Patish* (Aconitumheterophylum) is the drug of choice for indigestion, inflammation and respiratory ailments. Flower of *Bhoot kesh* is instant styptic. Root paste of *Hath Panja* (Dactylorhizahatageria) is applied as poultice on cuts and wounds and its extract is given in intestinal disorders. Roots and rhizome of *Ban Kakdi* (Podophyllumhexandrum) act as anticancer, antifungal and immunomodulator. Braham Kamals are found in rocky terrain above 4500 meters height. They are perfect fodder for sheep and wild goats alike. On my recent expedition to *Kundi* top, Nichar, I found a lot of them blooming magnificently amid bouldery morain, many eaten up by domestic or wild animals. Its scientific name is Saussureaobvallata and it is one amongst critically endangered species. In Tibetan medicine where it is named as Sah-du-goh-ghoo, entire flower is used for treating Uro-genital disorders, sexually transmitted diseases and relieving bone pain. *Hiun shella* leaves, when dried and powdered are used as aphrodisiac and improve potency.

Wildlife which I encountered during my sojourns to Rupi-Bhaba wildlife sanctuary, Pin valley National Park, Lippa-Asrang wildlife sanctuary or Rakchham-Chitkul wildlife sanctuary, were *Himalayan blue sheep/Ghoral* (Pseudoisnayaur), *Barking deer/ Kakkad* (Muntiacusspp.), *Himalayan black bear* (Ursusthibetanus), *Himalayan Red fox* (Vulpisvulpis), the *Lammergier* and *Red billed choughs*. We often heard stories of *Himalayan snow leopard* (Pantherauncia) and the elusive *Himalayan wolf/ Chenkhu* (Canislupuschanco), a canine of debated taxonomy, which often attack livestock, but we were not fortunate enough to have a glimpse except for their scats.

On one of our expedition to Nichar, *Chhot Kanda* top, local guide told us about some mysterious tribes living in the remotest of valleys up above, mostly inaccessible, indulging in agriculture practices on terraced land, but no one knew about them! In fact he showed us some terraced land, which may be artifacts, on a far ridge, which as per local belief belong to those fellows. More interiors one move, more mysteries and taboos one finds! And well, these common beliefs prove to be binding force in keeping people together. It wouldn't be an exaggeration if I say the local deity still wields the belief and trust of community. It is only due to sheer fear of *Devta's* curse that till today many forests are thriving and away from getting axed.

In Bhaba valley most of the high alpine pasture belong to *Devta Maheshwar ji*, Sungra. Shepherds are levied with appropriate fees to graze their livestock, on annual basis. But, as the tribal are becoming cosmopolitan with advancement of technology, the bastion of belief and devotion is shuddering a bit. No one will disagree that technology is needed for wholesome upliftment of entire society, be it in the deepest Himalayan ranges, but then this technology brings bane with itself.

Wildlife especially Barking Deer and Goral is vulnerable to poaching and are threatened due to habitat loss/ degradation as there is good network of roads and speeding vehicles, which will exacerbate the number of road kills.

Recent hydroelectric power project, above *Kafnu* at Bhaba Valley, Kinnaur, led to formation of motorable road towards Bhaba-Pin pass. The breath taking *Humti* trail which meander through thick forests and include steep ascent, is no more to be negotiated, for the road bypass whole the bottleneck. As we traversed through the *Gyaru* forest, below *Mulling* plains, I found the boulevard thinner than my previous jaunts, courtesy proximity to the road. As it is proposed that a motorable road would be constructed across Bhaba-Pin Pass to Spiti Valley, I wonder would the green zone recede further. Or would the next generation tread this beautiful road across cold desert to both side of the pass!

Making people aware about their environment and wildlife is desired at very early stage. Sensitization should take place at school level. Elder people must be made aware, for ifour irresponsible behavior towards wildlife remain unchanged, our coming generations won't be able to cherish these majestic creation of nature except digitally. Importance of forests should be inculcated in young minds for it's not just the firewood or furniture that these sylvan beauties bestow upon us but also the timely precipitation, protection from soil erosion, landslides and other natural calamities are also curtailed. Moreover the man – animal conflict will get minimized if forest remains conserved.

One must be abreast with the indigenous technical knowledge about wild medicinal herbs, those are found in high alpine pastures, so that well programmed emphasis is given to grow such plants in appropriate number without disturbing the ecological balance, as it will help local folk in elevating their economy and the mankind will be benefited at large.

Earnest endeavor should be made to develop alternatives to harvest these herbal plants that provide local people with equivalent income without damaging the delicate eco system. A thorough study about existing forages in high alpine pastures should take place and all its nutritional values should be evaluated. *In-situ* conservation through the establishment of nature reserve, *ex-situ* conservation through tissue culture and developing medicinal plant nurseries, conducting regular training on the procedure of medicinal plant collection, processing among the local people, traders and real stake holders should be prioritized.

Ways and means of improving the productivity and quality of pastures should be done, so that more quantity of forages gets cultivated on less land holdings and overgrazing curtailed, henceforth. Community should be sensitized to the level that they feel as if the forest estates are their own assets and they ought to be its saviors.

Those who are held responsible for violating the laws should be punished not only by the administration and Judiciary, but also need to be castigated and ostracize by whole community, for the deity doesn't thrive in small palanquin within the four walls of temple, but in the mind of hundreds of community people.

Glaciers and the Nomads

'It purportedly seems impossible to cross over'; my first words that I uttered to my hiking partner with utmost difficulty once we reached the pass.

It was a bright sunny day. No wafting fog or for that matter any swirling clouds were visible down the valley. What we could watch to the other side of the Pass were three beautiful emerald lakes which looked quite miniscule from this height but must be large one, once we get an opportunity to descend.

This terrain was quite familiar as we had already scaled the Pass two years ago. At that time we encountered many glaciers across the pass, even when it was the month of mid-August. And here we were again a month earlier this time, but to our dismay, no sign of any big glaciers. Even that big blue Ice, which pervaded towards *Bhaba* valley and culminated many streams, had shrunken considerably. Big appreciable crevasses and cracks were visible across its length and breadth. The only peak where thick coat of snow had wielded the scepter was the *Hans Bastion*. Or may be for it stood far away, we couldn't gauge its real fate as well.

Glaciers are the ultimate source of fresh water to huge civilization living down the valleys and further down in plains, and to amateur hikers like us, it provides the needed safety to cross the precarious passes.

It's not just the only reason that less snowfall last winter marred the situation, but those old dark glaciers which must have accumulated snow over hundreds of years, vanished gradually with considerable pace more so in last decade. Is it global warming or environmental change, we kept discussing. But one thing was sure, and we all agreed over it that the real beauty of a peak or mountain lies in its white cap and silvery braids.

And here this time we were sitting over a brown scary rocky terrain, rocks further petered by cold ice, that must have smothered it for centuries, making it too fragile to be relied upon in order to abseil down towards *Lippa* valley.

Recent research has suggested that local and regional air pollution may be speeding up the melting of glaciers at some places. Suit produced from burning of biomass and fossil fuel, land on ice and make it darker. Usually ice reflects the sunlight back, but once it become darker, more absorption of sunlight hence more melting.

As per one recent report, average global warming is 1.5 degree Celsius but on Hindukush Himalayas (the third Pole) it is around 1.8 degree Celsius and high elevation in mountain may see temperature rise more than 2 degree Celsius. During the warm summer months, meltdown from glaciers tends to run downstream and help replenishing nearby streams and rivers. Snowfalls during the winter months help build the ice back up again. But if glaciers are shrinking faster than they can rebuilt, the total amount of freshwater they can provide will ultimately decline and the rivers that they fed may start to dwindle. River basins are fed by both glacial melt water and rainfall from monsoon and in some places the monsoon are the more important source. Some research suggests that climate change may actually lead to heavier monsoon which could further accelerate the rate of melting ice.

Someone has rightly said, 'glaciers are like insurance policies which provide water when it is most needed during the dry season and during times of draught'. Because of the large contribution of monsoon rain, overall water flow across the entire region may not actually change much, and may remain relatively stable when considered on a large scale, but on specific location across the Himalayas which rely more heavily on glacier water may be in trouble. Communities at high elevation, located very close to mountain glaciers depend more heavily upon glacial melt water. Glaciers are important for secure water supplies, protect livelihood and prevent disaster across the region. Fresh water originated in cryosphere is essential for agriculture, hydropower, and inland navigation, cultural and spiritual purposes.

As we sat beside the sharp corniced ridgeline at *Lippu Khago*, deciphering the appropriate route, to cross over, all my thoughts were focused towards the denigrating glaciers.

It was not just the story of this deep valley only, in fact all high ranges and visible valleys reverberated the same story. Only grayish black demonizing peaks with intermittent clattering of the highly unstable boulders leading to rock fall were audible.

Glacial loss is difficult to predict over the Himalayas, as the rate of glacial melt depends upon number of variables including elevation and elevation dependent temperature, precipitation and debris cover among others.

One question which propped up my mind constantly was what happens when glaciers melt rapidly?

As per reports it is difficult to speculate how exactly the melting of the third pole's glacier will impact water flow and availability across the regions, that depends upon Himalayan rivers. This is because multiple factors influence water flow including monsoons. One effect that can be predicted is an increase in glacial lakes outburst floods (GLOFs).

In the year 2000, a massive flood was witnessed in the basin of river Sutlej, when *Par Choo* glacial lake in Tibet, suddenly burst and swept away countless roads, buildings, bridges etc, not to mention unfathomable loss of lives. Well, it is very difficult to predict individual GLOF's and it is clear that their frequency will go up as the climate warms. Glacial lakes across the Himalayas have increased in both number and size. But here as we stood over the Pass, we watched only three blue lagoons, just one more than what we appreciated two years ago while exploring this region.

Not all frozen water in the Himalayas is in form of glaciers. Glaciers are often referred to as rivers of ice, as they are large frozen volumes of water that slowly flow. Where there is less flow, but temperature remains below freezing, ice accumulate in the ground as permafrost.

Within the Hindukush Himalayas region study of the permafrost has been largely restricted to the Tibetan plateau beginning in the 1990's. Little research has been carried out in the rest of the region. The research on Tibetan plateau show that the active layer of permafrost is widening as it melts. We saw this phenomenon on *Parvati* glacier last year. This makes the ground less stable, leading to higher risk of landslides.

I was engrossed in these thoughts, while icy wind was more soothing than chilling at the Pass, a little bit of expected headache picked up. Billu wangpa appeared suddenly, for he *rekkied* the entire ridge and had found a comparatively safer place to get down towards the glacial lakes of *Lippa Khago*.

We repaired a big chorten, which must have been erected decades ago by the inquisitive shepherds and we tied Buddhist prayer flags, which were carried by Wangpa all the way.

'*Cairns (Stupas) are not just the repository of the Buddha's teachings but because of the powers they symbolize, guardians past which evil spirit can't proceed. With these stone spires gracing every major Himalayan Pass, Buddhist believe that negative forces would congregate in a particular valley and overpower the positive good forces. Also the prayer flags fluttering on the top of a Pass would carry all the positive energy across the valleys with gust, thus conquering the evil*', said Wangpa. He is much more spiritual than us!

Our plan was simple, first Billu will get down, explore the scree zone, if all seems fine, we will follow him; but if any difficulty encountered, he will come back and we will tie the rope and rappel down.

It was really a tough descent indeed. As Billu moved ahead, Badshah trailed him and gradually I dragged myself, using all limbs. It took almost an hour to reach the base after being struck in a narrow scree gully for twenty minutes. We celebrated safe descend by devouring fresh apples brought by Billu wangpa.

The glacial lakes were big indeed, as we saw massive old glaciers, feeding the lakes. Two of these lakes were interconnected, the second one filled with floating icebergs. There were many cracks in these glaciers, the fate same as of all other Himalayan glaciers. The lakes will be vanished, may be next time when we visit, say after a decade!

My headache wasn't mellowing down; the same condition was appreciated by Badshah. After walking for five minutes below the lakes, we saw three sheep dogs, running towards us. Badshah yelled instantly, "Hey look what we have got? Dogs! That means shepherd is around, let's move."

We were rejuvenated, merely by thought of taking some rest tonight at shepherd's place.

Down we saw a flock of goats grazing the green and the proud shepherd sitting calmly to the other side of a stream, wearing hallmark *Kinnauri* skull cap.

Ghuman Singh Negi was in his fifties, with tanned body, creased face, aquiline nose, chiseled jaw line, robust outlook and austere demeanor. He was into this profession for more than past three decades. As we sat beside him, we found that he was from *Nichar* valley and luckily his older brother was an ex-employee of our department. I had visited his home on the occasion of his superannuation a couple of years ago, though Ghuman was not present at that time, for he always weighed his solitude more blissful than social family affairs.

He was very much eager to host us and showed the trail down to his *dera*. We found another small blue lake, on our way down to shepherd's place.

Shepherd's life is always full of ecstasies, exhilaration, sacrifices, hard work and even some times horror. Ghuman Negi told us that he left his home when he was 15. He has been goading his flock to this pasture for almost last thirty years now. He has explored every deep valleys of this region, be it towards Spitior Kullu district. He was so much obliged to host us that he apologized for not having any dried mutton at his cache, and asked if we would like to relish *Pearls oyster*, even when he himself was a vegetarian. Badshah is also vegetarian. I had never ever devoured the much talked dish of shepherd's liking, the testicles, and it was being offered at such heights, how we could refuse that? The process of emasculation was carried out by Ghuman Negi himself, not clinical but dexterous one, as I witnessed closely.

By evening we were enjoying the last potion of *Old Monk*, under the starry night, of course the oysters were delicious indeed.

Next day we crossed a small and the only glacier beneath shepherd's hovel and marched towards the

Asrang village. Ghuman Negi led us all the way to next small pass magnanimously and showed the further trail. We were to cross two streams, he told cautiously, before 10am in any case, for they will turn into roaring torrents by noon.

We camped at the bank of *Gunzang* river that evening. Shepherd's hovel was visible to the other side. We couldn't dare to cross the makeshift, fallen tree bridge, for the gushing water was fiercely leaping over it at a few points.

After crossing it early morning next day, we met a young shepherd from *Rupi* valley. He was all alone in this camp as his partner had gone down the valley to bring essentials. Last night he kept scaring away the Himalayan brown bear, the biggest prey of livestock in this terrain. We had watched torch lights being flashed towards the mountain top last night and were right in guessing that some wild animal must have attacked the camp. He told that he has to move his camp soon as it was becoming difficult to scare the wild beast off.

Within a couple of hours we were at another stream called *Wari Khadd*. As the sunlight has melted the glaciers, the flow has increased manifold. Here we used our long rope to cross the torrent safely, for the frigid hip-deep water was strong enough to take us along. Our decision was right as we celebrated the victory with coffee and biscuits on a vantage point to the other side of river. This was the last river crossing.

As we ascended the countless hills *en route*, we met two younger shepherds. Both were camping individually. How they dwell all alone, we couldn't imagine.

Praveen Kumar, a teen cherubic faced boy from *Asrang* village was tending 300 goats all alone. He invited us to stay with him that night which we accepted gracefully.

That evening we talked about shepherd's nomadic life, their thoughts, their notion towards social life and all other aspects. He told us stories about his family, friends and off course a few encounters with wild animals. We could clearly watch the horror in his eyes. But he was content, blissful at the same time. A new Ghuman in making, I declared, tacitly.

While recalling his childhood, Praveen told us that he was never good in studies, and would often be punished by the teachers. With sparkling twinkle in his eyes, he however told us that he always liked the company of his father, while herding the ancestral livestock to nearby pastures. Once his father got seriously sick and he had to take care of whole flock at such tender age. He attained confidence of his family and now he is looking after his livestock all alone for past few years. He was just 14 years old.

Next morning he accompanied us up to nearby hill, *Kangaate Dhar*, the last ascent he assured, and bade us farewell only after taking mandatory *selfies*, for he would post them on his social media accounts once he retreat with his flock before the fall.

It was a perfect monsoon morning. Although sky was clear but the clouds were pervading above all the valleys beneath us. It seems as if we were at ethereal world.

Slowly the trail meandered along lush green pastures till the last descent across perilous rocky terrain and we saw first habitation after seven days. *Ho la se* (Thank you), we reached safely at *Asrang* village in *Lippa* valley. Well tarred road was visible and bus took us to district headquarters at *Rekong Peo*. Local people guffawed at us, for not many trekkers ventured towards *Lippu Khago* lately.

While sitting over the comfort of wheels, all I was thinking about was the prospect of nomadic shepherd's life, the resolute gaze of Ghuman Negi, the placid, twinkling eyes of young Praveen and of course the fate of receding glaciers. We must adhere to advises of experts, in order to save the glaciers and the future generations.

To slow down this abominable process of glaciers loss, we must focus on lowering carbon emissions. The challenge of preserving the cryosphere will increase if world warms at the current pace. Secondly, there must be constant observation and follow up of glaciers and permafrost melts. Relevant data sharing amongst all stakeholders should be done on regular basis, so that significant measures are adopted well on time, if need be. Thirdly improvement of research and observation should be used to anticipate disasters such as GLOFs and avalanches, and put process in place to minimize their impacts.

Epilogue

Hiking Sojourn: A Brief History

Being born in the Himalayan lap, it was but natural that we were brought up in its tradition and culture. For us mountains are like god that we revere and admire as it is the very core of our survival. Our ancestors have come up since time immemorial through the intricacies of these mountains, surviving the hardship that came through their way. When we were kids we use to accompany our parents and relatives to far flung areas; for gathering forages or to work in the fields. Tough times it used to be with no luxuries from today's perspective, but people were content with this hardship. Luxury is a comparative term though. Most of the time we use to cover the distance on foot; be it to attend the school or to work in far off fields.

Though, my native place showed signs of development comparatively earlier than other regions; for the Missionaries from Christian Missionary society opened a small mission station here at *Kotgarh* in 1843, in a Mess House of Army Garrison which was earlier stationed here. This was among few areas ceded by the Britishers from Maharaja of Punjab as per treaty after British-Gurkha war in the year 1815, in which the later were defeated. Apples were introduced to this region in the year 1916 all due to efforts of Samuel Evans Stokes later Satyanand Stokes.

People watched the lifestyle of westerners and took over the modern practices from them but still up to last three decades the aura was almost the same in terms of daily field works and journeys on foot, for the roads were being opened and means of transportation was much less.

I did my grad from State Agriculture University *Palampur* (HP) in Veterinary science, a profession dedicated to look after all other creatures than human beings. I love my profession for the reason that it is adventurous not only in terms of diagnosing the problem of a mute patient but to reach far flung areas to provide treatment to ailing creatures or to attend a disease outbreak at high altitude alpine pasture. The sense of excitement and exploration prevails all the time. Even the topography of my college was so much enthralling and serene that the mighty *Dhauladhar* ranges in the backdrop often used to be snow capped throughout the year. It infatuated all the residents and allured the hiking freaks in particular. A couple of time did we, so call adventure maniacs, tried to explore the high mountains but were finally content with merry making in the woods well below tree line.

My first serious hiking started in the year 2009 when I was posted at Govt. Veterinary Hospital Bahli a small picturesque place in Rampur sub-division of District Shimla, situated at about 7500 feet height just below the Great Himalaya ranges over hanged by white snow clad ridge of *Moral Dunda,* the alpine pasture.

It was an exigency call in the month of mid-August and monsoon was at its top. Due to heavy rain fall and high winds, trees of *Kharshu* (*Quercus semecarpifolia*) had fallen on the temporary sheds of *Gujjar* nomads whereby eight buffaloes succumbed to injuries and died on the spot. So, it was regarding verification of loss. A six to eight hour uphill hike led us to the spot. The beauty of the area could not be appreciated due to constant fog, and incessant rain made it hard to put each step forth. All that saved us from hunger was stuffed *Parathas* that my pharmacist, a local guy, stacked in his backpack from his home that morning. The first lesson was learnt,

'Always pack your rucksack with eatables as much as possible' to thrive the journey'.

Even the elderly looking *Gujjar*,supporting burgundy beards, was helpless at one point of time and told us that he won't be able to excel any further, rather we should retreat, for he would forfeit all the claims, which shows how unexpectedly harsh these hikes may be at times, even when he must have treaded these paths multiple times. We didn't camped at this beautiful *bugyal* / *Dunda* that night, for we never planned to do so and were lacking paraphernalia for the same, rather receded down to the base in pitch dark, fog smitten night as we astray the path but somehow managed to find the actual route after tiresome exercise. Second lesson was learnt,

'Always carry a source of light and try to remember the path, for once the fog shrouds the scene it's difficult to trace the unbridled path worst even at night'.

Our formal clothes were completely smeared with mud and filth and shoes were soaked up to the level of dripping. Lesson third,

'Wear appropriate attire with waterproof shoes'.

2012

- **Shrikhanad Mahadev (Kullu)**

After two years of my marriage, on a fine August morning, I got a call from my younger brother. It was regarding pilgrimage to *Shrikhand Mahadev.* I have heard a lot about this holy trek but never ever thought about accomplishing the same for I had never been kind of spiritual since my childhood. During this period a serial named *Man Vs Wild* featuring Bear Grylls was at its top on *Discovery Channel* and every youngster were enticed by it. I and younger brother used to mimic him in our field outings, so this journey was rather inspired by it for I was ecstatic about fantasies of surviving the journey to the top and back. I was not in the best physical shape at that point of time and neither inclined to usual jog and stretch up sessions. Ill equipped, ill-conceived, I agreed to proceed on this track for I thought as thousands of devotees of nearby villages visit this place every *Saawan*,(July-August, holy month for worshiping Lord Shiva as per Hindu rituals) what a big deal for us! With tennis shoes and one walking stick I accompanied the gang, all novices three in total. Little did I knew that the altitude of this peak is 5000 Plus and hypoxia was a literary term to me. As luck would have it, not even a single drop of rain did we encountered in this four days journey *via* the administration governed route of *Jaon*, *Nirmand*, District Kullu,(HP). But the headache that I encountered on the top would not dwindle ever in my memory.

'Always carry a first aid kit with necessary medicines before any hike'.

2015

- **Shrikhanad Mahadev *via* 12/20**

In 2014, I got transferred and posted at *Dutt Nagar* near Rampur Bushahar, on the banks of river Sutlej comparatively plane and hotter region, but the reveries of hiking mountains kept nurturing, more so in extreme summer, when temperature rose up to 40 degree Celsius. The cool pummels of icy winds that one encounter on higher altitude was a wistful thinking. In the year 2015, as luck would have it, I was asked to join another journey to Shrikhand Mahadev pilgrimage *via* a short but arduous trek through remote area of Rampur subdivision called 12/20. Vijesh Negi, my school mate and a local teacher of that area was the guide. Beside his teaching profession he is also an ardent hiker. He had scaled Shrikhand Mahadev peak four times up to now, through this tougher route. This was his fifth time and he invited me to join as duo, alpine style.

For he was well acquainted with the terrain and quite hardy being local to that area, so without a single thought I packed my rucksack; relinquishing the apple harvesting season back at home in the middle and left for *Ganvi,* the base camp. Vijesh is a strong lean guy with athletic built. He has changed little since our school days, a jovial fellow he is indeed.

We started the Hike early morning from his home amid monsoon drizzle with the hope that it would recede with time. As we muscled through thick forests of *Manjhbon* (middle forest, literally); rain only increased in intensity. We waited for some time in a makeshift shelter made for pilgrims but ultimately had to move, for the time was passing quickly and we had to reach one and only camp just 2000 meters vertically below Shrikhand peak, amid boulders and glaciers, which was maintained by the local shepherds. For I never followed the lesson learnt in previous journeys and didn't took my raincoat along, so everything was drenched including reserve clothes in my backpack. Also the DMS army shoes, which were not waterproof, were also dripping. Had it not been Vijesh who offered me his dry pullover at night, my journey would have been ended then and there.

Baar Ki Dhar is a steep ascent of almost five to six hours vertically, which is sufficient to break the back. Only local pilgrims dare to tread this route, for it is treacherous and not overseen by local administration unlike the alternate *Jaon (Nirmand)* route. That night we were only seventeen people in that camp and the eldest being me at 32. Next day weather cleared up and we were on the peak by 9 a.m. after starting from the base camp at 4:30 a.m. Only a handful of devotees were present there at that time. I did encounter that headache for quite some time. We headed down after spending a couple of hours, appreciating the wafting clouds well below us draping the valleys intermittently. In a single stretch we descended all the way down to Vijesh's home at *Ganvi*. Hot water shower was all that we needed. A strange sense of accomplishment prevailed, for we made it through more treacherous and arduous route, a feeling worth to be cherished till date.

It was only after this trek that I took up hiking as a serious affair.

'Start work out physically and mentally before any expedition'.

2016

- **Moraal Dunda, Chander Nahan (Shimla)**

Year 2016 remained largely as usual without any major hiking plans. A short jaunt up to *Moraal Danda,* a bugyalor grazing top, on which I wandered in the year 2009, a broad ridge which connects different valleys ofKinnaur, Rampur and Rohru region of District Shimla, HP. It was accomplished in the month of May. *Moraal Danda* trek is memorable due to persistent headache that I suffered at a height of mere 3600 meters not due to elevation but as a result of getting inebriated early morning while in the middle of gentle ascent in the sheer intoxication of brimming youth. I couldn't enjoy the beauty of that wild moor again this time, but one more lesson was learnt

'Never enjoy the summit or its trail with the maligned eyes of intoxication'.

A trek towards beautiful lakes of Chander Nahan was accompanishedin the month of June 2016. But it was also cut short due to unorganized pre-arrangements and comparatively large incoherent group. We had planned to cross over the pass into Kinnaur district and hired one young guide too, who would take us all along *Jot* (Pass) and show the trail down, but then we could make it only up to *Litham Thaach* and the beautiful seven lakes above it.

'Take a coherent, like minded group, with common goals for a hike'.

2017

- **Churdhar (Sirmaur)**

By year 2017 I had tried to become a serious hiker. I bought my own *three men plus* tent, a 60 liters Rucksack, good quality of trekking shoes and UV protective goggles all from *decathelon* store. The opening ceremony of my tent was below *Churdhar* peak. I have heard about this peak from my friends, being one of the highest peaks in the *Shivalik* ranges. So when I was asked to begin that year's summer hiking season with this peak, I agreed unhesitant. My younger brother, a Para-military man and an adventure lover, also joined the team with my two other professional colleagues and friends, Dr Jitender Verma and Dr Rohit Sharma, the spearhead of this tour.

We camped just below the *Shirgul Mahadev* shrine in *Churdhar* wildlife sanctuary, wondering how to set this new tent for it started to rain and we couldn't set our camp in time. After full night's rest amid incessant rain and thunderstorm, by morning weather was crisp and clear. Morning sunrise view was just awesome, like it is always at these heights. We reached the top, 3700 meters approx, after a moderate ascent of a couple of hours at around 11 am. One can see plainer region towards the south and snowy peaks of *Badrinath* and *Kedarnath* in *Garhwal* Himalayas towards north from the summit. This was our first night out independently with self cooked food and self established camp, a seed had been sown for upcoming expeditions.

'Keep the basic knowledge of any paraphernalia that one takes on any expedition'.

- **Kinnaur Kailash (Kinnaur)**

In July 2017 again I paired up with Vijesh (*Guruji*, I respectfully call him) as we had contrived to scale Kinnaur Kailash previous year. Two other batch mates, fitness freaks and wanderlust Jitendra Verma and Kanishak Sanjta also joined. I had been with these guys previous year on *Chander Nahan* trek, the region of seven lakes in the remote area of *Chirgaon* block of Rohru tehsil HP, far beyondlast village called *Janglik*. The fiasco that we met in that tour made us resolute to make this climb a success with short party and in alpine style. By this time I had joined the local football club at *Duttnagar,* Rampur Bushahar. Routine soccer sessions in big playground were being attended which was fun and worth it with regard to physical fitness. I had shed my extra lard and increased lung capacity appreciably. *Kinnaur Kailash* is considered to be tougher than *Shrikhand Mahadev.* A 6000 plus peak, its path is more treacherous than *Shrikhand Mahadev* and comparatively steeper, final climb of almost 1000 meters vertical, the hardest one. This time I had a raincoat, sleeping bag, and a tent in my backpack but couldn't find a perfect place to fix the tent and had to spend the night inside a cave, deep but only 3-4 feet high, which was really suffocating. Weather remained clear and we paid obeisance in early morning with Vijesh *Guruji* at the lead. We rested there for almost an hour before descending back. That headache was again appreciated on top and I had to take an aspirin. As we descended to lower altitude it was all gone, may be either due to the aspirin or altitude but I felt comfortable and led the group all the way down to the base camp.

- **Karra Pasture (Kinnaur)**

Towards the end of august 2017 an outbreak occurred in sheep flock that waskept on high alpine pasture at *Karra* in *Bhaba Valley* of District Kinnaur. I and another Vet, in-charge, Veterinary Polyclinic Rampur, Dr Suresh Kapoor, a local guy and affable, ardent mountain lover, was asked to march for examining the spot and submit the status report. It was a blessing in disguise to have an official tour towards beautiful *Bhaba* Valley and renowned *Bhaba Pin Pass.* At the outset I asked Dr Kapoor that given the weather condition, if all goes well we will try to cross over to *Spiti* Valley, to which he agreed. We camped at *Karra* Pasture for a week, examined the sick livestock, took samples and imparted the treatment. It was just awesome to camp at this height without any mobile signal, completely cut off from social life and enjoyed the pristine picturesque valleys of *Bhaba* region. Our pharmacists Mr. Rajeshwar Negi and Mr. Subhash Sharma were avid bibliomaniac and their tent that we occupied unwarranted, was stacked with books on various subjects that we referred in due course of time. Afternoons used to be reserved for discussions and planning session. Even today when we broach up the memories of those days we wander, on how many topics did we discussed nonchalantly in extreme length, for there was no other option to kill the time and playing cards was not our cup of tea.

One fine bright sunny morning, after sumptuous breakfast, we ventured out to explore a small hill adjacent to our base camp and to our surprise we saw the snow-capped *Jot/ Pass* for the first time. It infatuated us to the extent that we planned to crossover it in next 2-3 days.

Two of the shepherds of Animal Husbandry Department had crossed this *Jot* previously so they volunteer to come along. When all the preparations were done for early morning assault, (mess in charge took the pain of getting up as early as 3.00 am and prepared the stuffed *parathas* to be enjoyed on tour), by midnight weather took the turn and it started to rain unabated, which continued for next five days bringing snow at higher peaks. Temperature plummeted to freezing point. We waited for three days but then finally decided to recede as the magnitude of torrential rain only increased and we had to make ample preparation even to descend back to our home station. But the view of that pass was so enchanting that I dreamt of being at its top for many subsequent nights. For now the summer treks were over and I was hoping to make an assault as early as next summer.

'Wait for the right window to assault a mountain, for its not that you are always welcomed'.

2018

In the year 2018, I got transferred to Tribal region Kinnaur near to high Himalayan peaks of this area. Being posted particularly in this region where sheep and goat rearing is a tradition, means chances of some disease outbreak in high Alpine pasture in summer season. I attended three of them that year all in highly rough terrain of far-flung region of *Kumrang Valley* and *Bhaba Valley* both in Nichar tehsil. It was a hiker's delight for the beauty of these pastures increases manifold particularly in monsoon season with various color flowers blooming all across the wild moor.

- **Kinner Kailash Parikrama (Kinnaur)**

On our *Kinner Kailash* tour previous year, we had contemplated to perform *Kinner Kailash Parikramavia Charang* village, *a*n exhaustively daunting circumnavigation of mount *Kinnaur Kailash*. On short notice from Vijesh *Guruji,* as I was on the way back from attending an outbreak in *Kumrang* pasture, Rupi wildlife sanctuary, Kinnaur, I got ready for it. I was a bit tired but it acted as an appropriate acclimatization before crossing the *Charang La* (pass) which stood at 5300 meters. To me it was the toughest hike rather we have to clamber literally from the base of *La* to its top along treacherous moraine and glacial scree. Our class mate and a local guy Mr. Pradeep Negi was our guide. He is garrulous and jovial at the same time. this fellow is. He kept us giggling all the while with his funny talks.

We saw many Himalayan blue sheep (*Bharal*) in this trek, for this area is mainly influenced by *Buddhism* and the famous Rangrik *Tungma* monastery is situated here. To kill any creature is considered against the tenets of Buddhism hence the glorious wildlife is visible here all around. This time my backpack was loaded with gloves, headlamp, walking pole, torch, small Bluetooth speaker and many other accessories. After one night camping at *Lalanti* pasture, we accomplish the *Parikrama* without any big problem and that mandatory headache at 5300 meters wasn't appreciated at all.

- **Bhaba Pin Trek, Solo (Kinnaur – Lahaul Spiti)**

In the month of August 2018, my maiden solo trek of *Bhaba-Pin* pass was accomplished successfully. We had made all the preparations previous years to cross this pass along with my colleague Dr. Suresh. I had been to *Karra* pasture three or four times now and the deep valleys leading tothe base of thispass called *Fustirang*, lured me every time. My Rucksack carried all the required provisions and paraphernalia. Guided by the farm guy, who was stationed at *Karra* for grazing the livestock during summer season, we reached the top around 11 a.m. That final ascent above *Fustirang*, through narrow unbridled path was really breath taking. We prepared *prasadam,* as most of the shepherds supplicate to the God of mountains for their comfortable summer sojourns. Around Noon, I headed all alone to *Spiti* Valley, trailing local porters with their draft animals carrying luggage of some trekking group, which just passed ahead of us.

Their camping site was at *Mangrang che,* in the middle of cold dessert half way down to *Mudh* village. We reached there at 2.00 pm and they asked me to stay with them for that night. For it was sufficient day time left and I didn't felt exhausted, I continued to *Mudh*, all alone. Unmarked path meanders along the bank of river *Spiti* with intermittent ascent and descents.

I made a mistake though. I didn't f illed my water bottle just beneath the pass as a small stream of clear glacial water flowed through this valley all down to brown muddy water of *Spiti* river. I didn't found any fresh water stream up to almost 3 hours and the scorching sun in cold dessert, without any tree shade, was enough to dehydrate up to the level of daze. My backpack was full of eatables but more I ate, thirstier I felt. That day I literally felt that I may not die due to hunger but with thirst for sure. As

I saw some deep gorge from a distance, hope of some stream arose and my feet started to move fast, strides bit firmer. As I reached the gorge, I found gushing water all filled with glacial mud. It happened twice or thrice at every gorge. Finally exhausted, I sat beneath a big boulder providing shade from direct sunrays, beside a gushing *nullah,* with all hopes gone. And just then; as luck would have it, I saw a small black hose pipe dangling on the other side of *nullah* with fresh water drops trickling from it. I was elated to the extent that I threw my backpack aside and literally jumped to that place. It took almost 45 minutes to fill my bottle, but I drank ferociously as if to fill my every cavity. Now I was reassured that I am going to make it anyways. So one more lesson was learnt,

'Water bottle in your backpack should always be filled up to brim, no matter in which terrain you are travelling.'

An old man that I met near *Mudh* village *en route,* asked many questions inquisitively, most of which were like, why did I walk all the way this far? Why do people climb mountains? Didn't you find yourself lonely?

I smirked and kept mum, for I knew if I gave him an answer he won't understand anyways. I never felt alone, indeed all the while I was self introspecting, enjoying the views of cold dessert.

Finally I reached *Mudh,* last village of Pin Valley by 7:30 p.m. with daylight still prevailing. This *Bhaba-pin* pass expedition was a morale booster for me indeed; my physical and mental fitness was again proven beyond doubt. I must have carried rucksack weighing around 35 to 40 pounds all along this journey. This solo expedition only bolstered my future hiking plans and I was established as an amateur hiker in my small friend circle.

2019

- **Uttarakhand Himalayas**

In the beginning of the summers of 2019, we had planned to cross *Bhaba-Pin* Pass again, while I was to guide the small hiking group of friends, but due to heavy snowfall previous winter the Pass was closed up to the month of May 2019. So instead, we decided to explore *Uttarakhand* Himalayas. It was a pilgrimage route but we were more concerned about exploring the valleys of Kedarnath, Tungnath, Badrinath, Chopta, Hemkund Sahib and much talked, the Valley of flowers.

The best trek was from *Ghangaria* to *Hemkund Sahib* for it's not yet smitten with loud noise created by constantly hovering choppers like at Kedarnath and terrain is also picturesque with snow clad high peaks all around. At *Gurudwara Sahib* a big frozen glacial lake is situated in which like other pilgrims, I did performed holy dip as early as 7:00 a.m. It was mesmerizing aura towards the upper end of this trek, as bridled path switchback through huge glaciers. What I found most fantastic about Uttarakhand Garhwal Himalaya was steep vertical peaks, be it Kedarnath peak or Nanda Devi peak visible from *Auli.* I wished someday I would be able to scale a few of them!

- **Yula Kanda (Kinnaur)**

In the month of September 2019, on the holy day of *Janmashtami,* we headed towards *Yula Kanda,* Kinnaur, where the highest Temple of Lord Krishna in the world is situated. This is also the only Temple where idols of Lord Krishna and Lord Budha are kept on the same alter side by side, worshipped simultaneously by the pilgrims with utmost harmony. Where else do we find so serene environment? The beautiful ancient temple is built on a small island; surrounded by small Lake fed with glacial stream, with lots of cattle grazing around in high altitude pasture only to be taken back by villagers in the month of October – November, just prior to snowfall. On the holy festival of Janmashtami local devotees gather here en mass and celebrate the occasion with nightlong folk songs and local dance. Our guide in the trip was my colleague Dr. Ankush Sharma posted at the base of this *kanda,* a small picturesque village called *Urni.* We took the detour via *Urnikanda,* not so popular route, and had to make our way through thorny bushes and thick vegetation. It took us eight hours of arduous hike to reach the top only by 7 p.m. when the aura was shrouded by fog and all the pilgrims had left after previous night-long celebrations. It was good that the throng had dissipated making the environment serene but then to watch the traditional full night celebrations would have been blessing as well. We camped here for one night. It was difficult to prepare meals for we found kerosene stove really worthless at such altitude, as required pressure can't be produced in thin air, yet learning another lesson,

'Never carry a kerosene stove for camping above tree line, rather gas stove is helpful'.

- **Hamta Pass (Kullu-Lahaul Spiti)**

I was very much excited about exploring much talked Pin-*Parvati* trek. Ienquired about the number of days needed and status of hike from Billu Negi, an avid trekker from *Bhaba* valley, who became my friend lately, for we had common likings on many things, exploration in particular. He shared a contact with me for this*Pin-Parvati* trek. I talked to this guy from Kullu, Heera Bhai, who was ready to guide us through this Pass, which would take at least seven to eight days. But then I couldn't find serious members for this sojourn. I befriended with Hira bhai, a typically Kullu localite, a well established guide. He must have recognized my zeal for hiking so he told me if I could join hiking party from Malaysia in late September, which would hike *Hamta* pass from Manali. I got ready instantly.

The Pass was accomplished successfully and I learnt a lot many things, after watching closely the guided hikes and its professional aspects.

2020

- **Bhaba Pass, Lippa Pass, Kundi Top Nichar (Kinnaur)**

In the summers of 2020, amid COVID pandemic, only local hiking in Kinnaur district could be accomplished. It was lock down condition throughout the summers and local people were scared to allow any outsiders. Ten days twofer, along *Bhaba-valley* were mesmerizing, especially *Bhaba-Lippa Khago*, this wasn't ascended even by local folks for quite some times. It was a true exploration for us. Though we couldn't cross over to *Lippa* village due to Corona restrictions, but we sat a high camp at 4800 meters, the highest ever for us, of course, till that year.

In the month of September, an assault over *Kundi* top, *Nichar*, Kinnaur was done along with local women, the first ever experience to hike with opposite gender. Many whims about womenfolk were quelled hereupon.

'Women are equally strong given the appropriate opportunity'.

2021

- **Belnu-Bashal Top (Kinnaur-Shimla), Bhaba-Pin-Parvati (Kinnaur-Lahaul Spiti-Kullu)**

In the last summers of my Kinnaur posting, yet another attempt to ascend *Tirmi top* (above *Taranda* village, Kinnaur) was made successfully, but this time we explored the valley deep, eastward upto *Belnu* mountain and westward to *Bashal* top and further down to Sarahan, Rampur. It was mostly shepherd's trail that we tread, but the besotted beauty of this alpine pasture is inexplicable. It also acted as acclimatization work for high Passes expedition thereafter.

Bhaba-Pin-Parvati trek included two high, 5000 plus Passes. It was only two men expedition, and none of us had ventured towards Parvati Pass before. Shakara Khago, is a non-conventional Pass, where only a few rock solid trekkers must have headed, but mostly its local shepherds who graze their animals to the farthest of these valleys. It took us ten days to complete this jaunt, and circumambulated three districts namely Kinnaur, Lahaul Spiti and Kullu.

'Always carry a rope, for river crossing shouldn't be taken so lightly'.

2022

- **Moraal Dunda (Shimla)**
- **Bhaba-Lippa circuit (Kinnaur)**
- **Rupin Pass (Kinnaur-Shimla)**

In the second fortnight of June 2022, when the lower altitudes were simmering with unabated heat wave, we decided to scale our local bugyal, Moraal Dunda. Though I had been to this alpine pasture twice before, the fascinating aura of high altitude only allure you every summer. This time we explored the valleys further up to Ransaar valley of Chirgaon sub-division and also witnessed the dreaded serracs of the *Nardi* mountain ranges.

In the month of July 2022, the half left task of crossing over the Lippa Pass was accomplished. We had been upto this Pass in CORONA era, but now, as the restrictions were over, it was perfect time to explore down the Lippa valley. Against our convictions, this year there was no glaciers to cross the Pass easily and it was not just simple descend all the way down to Lippa valley. We had to cross two fierce glacial rivers and scale many small hills before the final switchback down to beautiful Asrang village.

'It's not always an easy descend once you cross the pass, for summiting a Pass is only half the journey.'

In mid September 2022, we hiked to the Rupin pass, starting our journey from Sangla village Kinnaur and reached Jakha village in District Shimla. This was just opposite to the normal route operated by various trekking companies. We hired a guide from Sangla, only up to the pass that also on the behest of my concerned partners, through a common contact. We never talked about the fees till last moment, for we thought it would be nominal. Surprised we were only at the pass when the charges asked were exorbitantly high. But we were not in a position to argue, for it was our own mistake to take the things lightly. Anyhow, the vista was mesmerizing though my partners were in a hurry to conclude the journey at the earliest, against my volitions. It was a kind of mixed feeling, for we concluded the journey in just two daysand appreciated the life in remotest habitation.

'Always have the contract at the start of journey, never take things lightly and for granted. There is money mystique even in the mountains too

……and the journey still continues.

Acknowledgements

This book is not merely a piece of literature, but a journey indeed; which would not have been accomplished all alone.

I owe my deepest gratitude not only to various expedition members, but to a lot of my friends and family members for encouraging me and supporting me through the whole writing process.

I feel extremely lucky to have Dr. Shalmali Thakur, my good friend and colleague as my first editor. Without your belief in my work and constant motivation to scribble every sojourn, and patience through the editing process, this piece of work would never have come to existence at very first place.

I am indebted to many people who have helped me directly or indirectly along the way, as I travelled to various parts of the Himalaya. Special thanks, alphabetically to, Boris Kulwinder, Bisht Anuraj, Drs. (Jitender Verma, Suresh Kapoor, Pramod Mahajan, Ankush Sharma, Pooja Rathaur, Saru, Bindu Negi, Vikas Ranta, Rohit Sharma), Heera Lal, Joshi OP, Kaushal GS, Kumar Ashok, Kumar Praveen, Martyn Kuldeep, Navvaal Narender, Nanta KC, Negi Bittu, Negi Ghuman Singh, Negi Pradeep, Negi Vipin, Olga Suneel, Parshetka Vijesh, Sanjta Kanishak,

Sharma Naresh, Shiv Kishore, Thakur Sanjeev, Vijay Laxmi and Wangpa Billu

I would like to thank my younger brother Pawan 'Johnny' for always being my designated reader and encouraging every time not only for some big expedition but to ink them on papers too.

I also owe gratitude to Naveen K. Kharyal, who gave important tips regarding publishing this book.

And of course, this book is for you Mom, wherever you are, thanks for being You, free and resolute. You are always an inspiration, a part of me.

My Dad, for bearing me unconditionally, despite the rebel I have been.

And lastly, my better half, Ranjana, for without your tacit support, I would have but lived a vegetative life, what so ever large it might have been.

Glossary

Aate – Big brother

Antakshari – A play in which participants/ teams sing a song

Baudi – Natural source of water

Bhaado – Sixth month of Nanakshahi calendar (late august to late September)

Bugyal – A wide spread lush green pasture

Chalamat – To form a *cul de sac* with both hands

Dera – A temporary shed made by nomads

Dhar – Ridgeline of a particular valley

Dhaank – Perilous rocky terrain

Dhoop – Incense

Dhulle Maah – Split and dehusked black gram lentils

Dogri – Far flung fields, which are inhabited seasonally

Fulyari – Of flowers

Ghasani – Waste land on which forage is grown

Ho-La-Se – Thank you

Jadi – Roots

Jawan – Youth/ army personnel

Jhulla – A basket shaped seat hanging by two ropes or chains from a metal frame, commonly used to cross the river

Jomparing – Hell

Jot – Pass

Kadwi – Bitter

Kanda – High pasture land above human habitation

Kero-stove – A normal household stove which uses kerosene as fuel

Khadd – A seasonal gushing deep gorge

Khago – Pass

Kutcha – Not paved

La – Pass

Malka – Red split dehusked lentils

Maam – Maternal uncle

Moori – The first distillate

Nabu – Himalayan blue sheep

Nullah – A seasonal small stream

Pabang – Valley

Pratishta – To sanctify

Pul – Bridge

Rekkie – Reconnaissance

Riyasat – Kingdom

Saat Mai – Seven Holy Mothers

Saawan – Fifth month of Nanakshahi calendar (Mid July to Mid August)

Shakhare – Pile of pebbles or stones

Stupa – Buddhist shrine

Thaach – Lush green moor

Suggested Readings

Ajay, Shukla. *The Trails less Travelled*, Niyogi Books, 2015

Anatoli, Boukreev & G. Weston De Walt. *The Climb*, PAN Books, 2002

Bill, Aitkin. *Footloose in the Himalayas*, Permanent Black, 2003

Ed, Viesturs. *No Shortcut to the Top*, Broadway Books, 2006

Ed, Viesturs. *K2*, Broadway Books, 2006

Frank S, Smythe. *The Valley of Flowers*, Speaking Tigers, 2015

Gaurav, Punj. *The land of Moonlit Snows*, Tranquebar, Westland Publications, 2018

Jack, London. *The Sea Wolf*, Bantam Classic, 2007

Joe, Simpson, *Touching the Void*, Vintage Books, 1988

Joe, Simpson. *The Beckoning Silence*, Vintage Books, 2002

Jon, Krakauer. *Into the Wild*, PAN Books, 1998

Jono, Lineen. *Into the Heart of the Himalayas*, Speaking Tiger, 2020

Peter, Matthiessen. *The Snow Leopard*, Vintage, 2010

Ravi, Manoram. *When the Road Beckons*, Ravman Books, 2005

Reinhold, Messner. *My Quest for Yeti*, PAN books, 2001

Robert, Macfarlane. *Mountains of the Mind*, Vintage Books, 2004

Sir Francis, Younghusband. *Wonders of the Himalaya*, Srishti Publications, 2000

Shivya, Nath. *The Shooting Star*, Penguin Books, 2018

Slawomir, Rawicz. *The Long Walk*, Robinson, 2007

Stephen, Alter. *Becoming a Mountain*, Aleph Book Company, 2014

Stephen, Alter. *Wild Himalaya*, Aleph Book Company, 2019

www.ingramcontent.com/pod-product-compliance
Lightning Source LLC
LaVergne TN
LVHW041157150826
845673LV00001B/191